PLANNED INNOVATION

Second Edition

A Dynamic Approach to Strategic Planning and the
Successful Development of New Products

by

Frank R. Bacon, Jr.
Professor of Marketing
Michigan State University

and

Thomas W. Butler, Jr.
Vice President, Engineering & Research
AMF, Inc.

Industrial Development Division
Institute of Science and Technology
The University of Michigan
1981

Reprinted 1986

Available from

Industrial Development Division
Institute of Science and Technology
The University of Michigan
2200 Bonisteel Blvd.
Ann Arbor, MI 48109

Printed in the United States of America

ISBN 0-938654-32-2

Foreword

During the past twenty-five years Dr. Bacon and Dr. Butler have maintained an active professional interest in new product development. They have achieved an insight into the process from almost every logical perspective: both authors have held full-time positions in industry; yet they have also supervised university research on the subject, have taught graduate-level courses, and have given seminars for industry on strategic planning and new product development. In addition, they have frequently combined their special talents to work as consultants to dozens of firms interested in developing new products. In his present capacity as corporate vice president of engineering and research for AMF, Inc., Dr. Butler is presently assisting some fifty divisions in new product development and associated research.

The authors initially used the procedures outlined on the following pages primarily in industries and product fields involving high technology, including: electronic computer main frame and peripheral devices; electronic and electromechanical components; industrial controls for machine tools; scientific instruments; automotive components; optical coatings; building supplies and equipment; materials-handling equipment; snowmaking equipment; and waste treatment equipment. Since the first edition of this book was published, the authors have expanded their work to include a number of consumer products, especially those in the recreational equipment field, such as bicycles, skis, golf clubs, boats and marine accessories, etc. Their work has also encompassed military aerospace products, traffic signals, medical equipment, and components for the appliance industry to mention a representative few.

As a team, they are uniquely qualified for their work. Dr. Bacon holds a Bachelor's degree in Electrical Engineering from Purdue University and Master's and Ph.D. degrees from The University of Michigan, where he specialized in marketing and quantitative research methods. He was formerly director of the research program for the Industrial Development Division of the Institute of Science and Technology and is now Professor of Marketing in the Graduate School of Business at Michigan State University.

Dr. Butler's training is exclusively in engineering. He received all degrees—B.S., Master's, and Ph.D.—in Electrical Engineering from The University of Michigan. Formerly Professor of Electrical Engineering at The University of Michigan and Director of the Cooley Laboratory, a major electronics research laboratory in the University, serving both industry and government, Dr. Butler is now corporate Vice President of Engineering and Research at AMF, Inc., as mentioned above.

In the summer of 1971 the authors first presented the philosophy and procedures of their approach to new product development at the Management Briefing Seminars sponsored by the Institute at Traverse City, Michigan. The interest in having a written statement of their methods was so strong that the Institute sponsored the preparation of the first edition of the present monograph.

As was the case with the original monograph, the revised edition is not a research study. It is, rather, a statement of the authors' philosophy of approach to strategic planning and new product development.

However, the revised edition attempts to offset the earlier omission of quantitative and illustrative data to support the approach, which was unfortunately necessary with the original monograph, because much of the authors' work had been done recently with individual firms on a confidential basis.

This revision also gives greater treatment to consumer product planning, showing the necessary contrast in methods used for each type of product. The companion cases also illustrate both consumer and industrial product development.

The addition of the illustrative materials reinforces the persuasive logic of the procedures suggested by the authors, which are based on years of successful empirical testing in many firms. We feel the more expanded illustration will enable the procedures to be even more useful to other firms as well.

The Industrial Development Division is a unit of the Institute of Science and Technology of The University of Michigan. The Division was established to accomplish two of the purposes of the Institute as stated in the Bylaws of the Board of Regents of The University; namely, "to serve as a center of science and technology," and "to encourage, support, and conduct research in all fields of pure and applied science, engineering, and technology, which are potentially important to future business and industrial development of the State of Michigan. . . ." An important phase of the Division's research program has been the study of various Michigan industries, their relation to similar industries elsewhere in the nation and abroad, and the effect of modern science and technology on these industries. Such studies aid in the improvement of the competitive position of Michigan companies as well as contribute to the general industrial development of the State.

In addition to carrying on research and publishing the results of such industrial studies, the Division sponsors seminars and workshops for industry and maintains a liaison service to promote the flow of information between faculty and research groups within the University and industrial firms.

Joseph J. Martin
Acting Director
Institute of Science & Technology

Acknowledgments

The authors wish to acknowledge and express their appreciation to our colleagues E. Jerome McCarthy, Adjunct Professor of Marketing, Michigan State University, and to our Associates Joseph E. Szalay and R. Trezevant Wigfall, all of whom read the manuscript and made many helpful suggestions.

The authors also express appreciation to the many firms which permitted case materials to be included and assisted in their preparation: AMF, Donnelly Mirrors, Lear Siegler, Pillsbury, N.A.Taylor Co., Toledo Scale Division of Reliance Electric Company, and Votrax Division of Federal Screw Works.

In addition, thanks are also due to our editor, David Peelle of the Industrial Development Division and to Patricia Rapley, who typed numerous drafts of the manuscript.

Frank R. Bacon, Jr.
Thomas W. Butler, Jr.

TABLE OF CONTENTS

SECTION ONE: THE PROBLEM AND THE APPROACH

SECTION TWO: STRATEGIC PLANNING PROCEDURES

LIST OF TABLES

LIST OF FIGURES

SECTION ONE

THE PROBLEM AND THE APPROACH

Chapter 1

The New Product Development Problem

New products are the lifeblood of any firm. Without them, opportunities for corporate growth and profitability are greatly reduced. Yet, traditionally, the failure rate for new products has been quite high.

In the classic study of new product development made almost 30 years ago, Booz, Allen, and Hamilton found that only two out of ten products became a commercial success and that seven out of eight hours of technical effort failed to become commercially successful.[1]

Despite a general recognition of the seriousness (in terms of time and monetary expenditures) and the pervasiveness of the problem, a high percentage of new products failures persists throughout industry today. Why? What are the roots of the problem? Simply these—even though the complexity of man's existence is constantly increasing, many firms cling to myths regarding new product procedures. Despite the recognition that what is new today may be obsolete tomorrow, most firms are inadequately equipped to deal with rapid change. Unfortunately, they may be doomed to mediocrity and perhaps a premature demise. We will first look at technological change in its historical perspective and then consider the myths regarding new product procedures.

Technological Change: A Recent Historical Perspective

The accelerating rate of technological change may be roughly measured in a variety of ways. One measure might be speed of transportation (see Figure 1.1). Our early ancestors could walk or run at an average speed of 3 to 5 miles per hour. The horse-drawn carriage allowed man to accelerate to about 10 to 15 mph.

It was not until 1850 and the advent of the steam locomotive that travel speed approached 50 mph. From the middle of the last

3

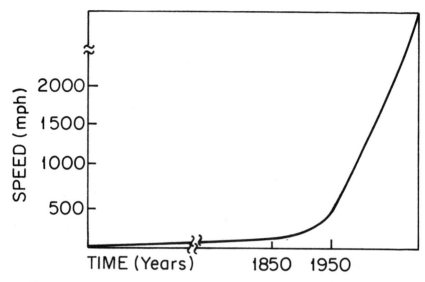

Figure 1.1 *Speed of Transportation Over the Last 50,000 Years.*

century there were additional incremental increases in the speed
of transportation, until in 1950 a speed of approximately 350 mph
was reached.

Since 1950, commercial speeds ranging up to 1,000 mph have
been achieved, and speeds of 2,000 mph have been experi-
mentally reached. If rocket flights to the moon are considered in
the general transportation category, speeds in excess of 25,000
mph have been achieved.

It took man, in other words, thousands of years to reach a
travelling speed of just 50 mph. In a mere 100 years, however,
those 50 miles were increased sevenfold to 350 mph. What is
more, in the thirty years since 1950, man has multiplied his travel
speed potential by somewhere between 500 and 1000 percent.

A similar curve depicting the rate of man's total technical
achievements over the last 50,000 years would also show explosive
increases since 1950. For example, think of changes in medicine,
communications, or computational abilities. Rapidly accelerating
developments in technology have greatly altered the pace and
practice of business since World War II, just as they have altered
the speed of commercial travel as shown in Figure 1.1.

The pace of technical change has both broadened the scope
of choices and increased the sophistication of application of tech-

nology for every industry. The result is that research and development decisions in product design are infinitely more complex than they were a generation ago.

Machine tool firms, long accustomed to leisurely change, must almost overnight assimilate the technology of computer control and such new methods of measurements as laser metrology. In like manner, the small manufacturer of remote-access computer terminals must now be able to make a wise selection from many alternatives in solid-state logic, memory, and keyboard devices.

As everyday experience shows, the possibility clearly exists that a company will unwisely commit its technical resources to a poorly defined product, or that the technology selected will be outdated by the time the product has reached the marketing stage. The costs from efforts wrongly directed can turn out to be exorbitantly high, creating an economic catastrophe for the smaller firm and a severe profit hazard for the well-established larger one.

Why have many firms not adopted suitable new procedures to guide product developments in this era of unprecedented opportunity and technological risk? We feel, in large part, that the answer lies in the fact that many firms still cling to old myths regarding new product procedures.

In the following sections, we will describe three prominent myths and explain the consequences or problems resulting from their conscious or unconscious acceptance.

Myths Regarding New Product Development

After 25 years' experience working with many firms producing industrial, commercial, and consumer products we have found that tacit acceptance of three myths underlies most of the problems encountered in trying to achieve successful new product developments.

Almost everyone has heard of the first one—the "better mousetrap." This myth says that all you have to do to succeed in business is "to build a better mousetrap and the world will beat a path to your door." Most examples cited in support of this myth represent major technical breakthroughs associated with a wide and intense demand for the product. For example, the electric light bulb, the telephone, the radio, and television.

The second myth, which we call the myth of "another Xerox," might be considered the first cousin of the "better mousetrap" myth. This myth might be expressed as follows: the only worthwhile goal of the new product development function is to find the "super" product, a product so wonderful, its technology so powerful, its patent so strong, and its market so large that growth and profits are virtually automatic. The director of new products is told, "Find us another Xerox," because management believes that the firm cannot be a truly great commercial success unless it finds such a product.

The third myth, "the gift of genius," is perhaps a second cousin of the myth of "another Xerox." This myth argues that successful new products result only from a "gift of genius," that special inner vision that allows one to grasp in a twinkling all the essential aspects of a new product. Land, and his invention of the instant camera, is a typical example cited by supporters of this myth. It emphasizes that all a firm has to do is to find the right person, "turn him loose in the lab," and successful new products will begin to flow immediately.

Problems Stemming from the Myths

All of these myths are deceptive because they contain some grain of truth—at least one example that seems to prove the rule. In every instance, however, they do not tell the whole story. In a mathematical sense, there are many more examples that disprove them.

Problems with "The Better Mousetrap"

The myth of "the better mousetrap" is perhaps the most insidious of the three, because it leaves so much unsaid. It assumes that the world has a strong *need* for the "better" mousetrap (and "better" is often undefined). Regardless of how good the mousetrap is, however, the world will not beat a path to the door unless there are many mice to be caught. Thus, most examples cited for the appropriateness of the "better mousetrap" myth presume the existence of a widespread and deeply felt need, understood by the creator of the new mousetrap.

Also the "better mousetrap" myth does not consider whether the world will *buy* the better mousetrap at a price high enough to cover total cost and leave an attractive profit! Furthermore, it assumes that somehow the world will find out about the better mousetrap, presumably by word of mouth.

Yes, there is truth in this myth, but it has led many a would-be independent inventor astray. Most often we find that the independent inventor has very little understanding of the market requirements (live trap or death trap) or the size of market for the product, or the cost of competing products or devices. In almost every instance we have seen, it has been the lack of understanding of market needs that has led to failure from such independent efforts. Many brilliant and well-meaning inventors are being misled by the "better mousetrap" myth every day.

Problems with "Another Xerox"

The concept that every product development activity should direct its efforts toward finding the one "super" product, "another Xerox," tends to misdirect the efforts of the product development function. There can be no doubt that finding "another Xerox," which meets a large pent-up demand at competitive prices, might lead to considerable commercial success. However, no one would doubt the improbability of most firms achieving success this way. Perhaps more importantly, however, significant commercial success *can* be achieved in another way with much higher probability—through a series of intelligent, but more modest new product developments.

The fact that history has shown that most successful firms have done so *without* "another Xerox" should not be surprising. Throughout the history of technological progress, major breakthroughs have been shown to result from a *series* of lesser events. Very often the breakthrough, even though it was made possible by the efforts of many others, is credited to the person who refined or perfected the concept, and who appeared fairly late in its evolution. Recall that Marconi is generally considered the father of wireless telegraphy because he obtained the first patent in 1896. However, the body of technical knowledge that Marconi organized to produce the first practical systems of wireless telegraphy was actually the result of many scientists who had been working

7

for years on developments associated with radio transmission and reception.

Let us consider a more recent example. In 1966 the Department of Defense published a study of events leading to major increases in the performance/cost of a number of military weapons systems. The investigators concluded, "the most significant finding is that in the weapons systems studied, large changes in performance/cost are the synergistic effect of many innovations, most of them quite modest."[2] It is not surprising that most commercial successes stemming from new product developments follow the same pattern.

We have observed a corollary pattern when dealing with product changes in mature markets. In such instances, a *small* increase in *technical* performance of the product may have *great commercial* significance. For example, the Hogan Golf Company was able to reduce the total club weight less than 10 percent while maintaining the same swing weight with its "Legend" shafted clubs. The commercial result of this relatively small technological improvement enabled Ben Hogan to more than triple their sales in three years and move to number one in sales of golf clubs by pro shops.

In preparing for the 1978 defense of the Little America's Cup, the designers (and racers) of the Class C catamaran approached AMF for assistance in developing lightweight structures for their new catamaran. In working with these designers, AMF learned that a three to five percent performance (speed) advantage over competition would give the U.S. team a tremendous advantage in the challenge cup races. That speed advantage, obtained with AMF's assistance, enabled the U.S. team to sweep the series from the Italian challengers in four straight races. The recognition of the importance of a small percentage increase in the speed of such sailboats led AMF to develop new lightweight structures which ultimately will improve the design of its entire line of sailboats, cruisers, and yachts. AMF has already succeeded in reducing the superstructure weight of its 58-foot Hatteras Motor Yacht (shown in Figure 1.2) by 25 percent. This improved fuel efficiency, reduced production cost, and provided more room for customer options to be installed.[3]

The myth of "another Xerox" does great disservice to reality, since it diverts undue attention to the improbable instead of focusing attention on the commercially and technically probable. A firm's success is most likely to be related to understanding how modest product modifications and additions can meet real customer needs.

Problems with the "Gift of Genius"

The "gift of genius" myth asserts that all you have to do to succeed with new products is to find the right person and give him time to invent products. Unfortunately, even if such a highly qualified technical person is found, the approach is almost surely doomed to failure, because it does not emphasize the central importance of developing products which meet market needs. For example, a number of years ago we provided assistance to a small firm in the scientific instrument field which had hired a very competent director of research and development—with exactly this approach in mind. Within a few months many new product developments had been started. As the costs of developing all the ideas to completion rose, the firm realized it could not make the decisions regarding which products to fund without a better

Figure 1.2 Hatteras 58-foot Motor Yacht.

understanding of market requirements. After a market-oriented approach was installed, the number of projects under way was reduced dramatically, and the more concentrated effort on a small number of better-defined developments led immediately to significant growth in sales and profits for the firm.

The "gift of genius" myth also implies that systematic procedures are of no value in new product development, since the flash of genius is the prime ingredient required. The myth implies that ordinary mortals need not attempt the activity for they are doomed to failure. The myth discredits the long hours of methodical work and perseverance typical of even the greatest early inventors, such as Edison. And it ignores the reality of modern-day technology, where major new developments often result from combinations of advances from many unrelated technical fields, requiring teams of experts from different disciplines for the successful integration.

The myth thus fosters the misconception that systematic procedures cannot be developed and applied to the new product development activity. We have found in many instances that firms did not even consider seeking such procedures simply because they did not feel that new product activity *could* be systematized, that the management of such activities was, at best, strictly an intuitive affair.

Three Keys to Solution of New Product Development Problems

Over the years, we have found three keys to the solution of the many problems stemming from belief in the myths described above. These keys, shown in Figure 1.3, are: (1) to obtain in-depth understanding of market needs before proceeding with technical and market developments, (2) to focus on innovation instead of invention, and (3) to use systematic and efficient procedures in all phases of new product activities.

Obtaining In-Depth Understanding of Market Need Before Major Expenditure

Many of the problems created by belief in any of the three myths can be avoided simply by insuring that all new product

KEYS TO SOLUTION OF NEW PRODUCT
DEVELOPMENT PROBLEMS

1. Obtain in-depth understanding of market need.

2. Focus on *innovation* instead of *invention*.

3. Use systematic and efficient procedures throughout process.

Figure 1.3

developments are based on an in-depth understanding of market need. If this were done, many inventors would not waste their life savings on a product idea that has no real demand, all the while thinking that they would succeed by developing a "better mousetrap." Firms which understand the commercial significance of modest technical advances in products, need not devote unreasonable resources toward achieving the improbable "another Xerox" in order to be successful. Today's generation of miniature pocket calculators is the result of many technical achievements, each of which provided the foundation for an earlier calculator, most of which were themselves commercially successful.

Futhermore, firms which understand the market need for products can also better understand how resources and personnel can be organized to systematically resolve the development problems without sole reliance on a "gift of genius." The first conquest of Mount Everest was as much the result of careful planning and logistical support as it was the result of selection of personnel, advancements in equipment, timing, and courage. And the top was reached by putting one step in front of another, not by one single bound.

The central importance of understanding market need is supported by much collaborating evidence. During the past decade or so a number of investigations have been made of the innovation process. Among these, six independent and quite diverse studies identified one common factor leading to success in new product innovation: the proper identification and measurement of (customer) needs.[2,4,5,6,7,8]

Working in the mid-1950's as research engineers developing new products for military electronic countermeasures, we observed the crucial importance of such proper need identification and began developing techniques to determine product requirements for military products.[9,10,11] Following this work, the first use of our procedures in nonmilitary products came in 1958–1960 to guide new product developments in the embryonic computer field.[12] Over the ensuing years, our techniques have been refined through application and testing in many firms and types of industries.

During the process of refinement, we have learned that most firms make some effort to define needs, but typically do not analyze the product requirements *in sufficient depth* either qualitatively or quantitatively to provide positive guidance to subsequent technical development and marketing activities. Often, well-meaning personnel simply do not know how to determine and specify the requirements, or they use improper tools, which produce misleading results, which, in turn, compound the problems. The procedures we have developed for identifying and measuring need (product requirements) represent the cornerstone among the various building blocks of the Bacon-Butler approach to planned innovation.

Focusing on Innovation Instead of Invention

We have identified the second key to successful new product development as recognizing that the objective is to innovate, not solely to invent. The distinction (shown in Figure 1.4) is that an invention is merely a solution to a problem, often a technical one; whereas an innovation is the *commercially successful use* of this solution (invention.)[13,14] From the start, the new product development activity must focus on insuring that any products developed will be commercially successful. Recall that acceptance of the "better mousetrap" myth results in inventing a device without regard to

---

INNOVATION VERSUS INVENTION

INVENTION   = Solution to a Problem

INNOVATION = Commercially Successful Use of Invention

Figure 1.4

its commercial success. By examining all aspects of the innovation before major expenditures on development, such as market need, technical, production, and marketing requirements, and a basis for protection from competitive inroads, the potential problems stemming from the myths are addressed immediately. The key is simply to focus on the innovation—commercial success—from the beginning rather than merely on the invention.

Use of Systematic and Efficient Procedures

The third key to successful new product development is to use systematic and efficient procedures in all phases of the process. Such procedures insure that the pitfalls of "a better mouse-trap" will be avoided, and that opportunities can be selected, evaluated and developed without reliance solely on "a gift of genius" or the objective of finding "another Xerox."

We have developed a number of procedures to integrate all aspects of product development activity into one efficient, co-ordinated process. A series of later chapters is devoted to these procedures.

One of the fundamental difficulties with new product innovation is the inherent complexity of the task. It requires information and coordination and, usually, manpower support from diverse and often conflicting interests—marketing, research, development and engineering, manufacturing, and finance. For example, a product that has superior physical design characteristics may still fail because of high manufacturing costs, inadequate quality control, poor service, or inadequate and poorly timed marketing operations. Later we shall address organization, staffing, funding, and review processes needed to accomplish the coordination and control of the total innovation process.

Conclusion: Improved Procedures Can
Solve The Problem

The fact that major problems exist in managing the new product innovation process is well-known today. The accelerating rate of technological change demands that improved procedures be used to increase the efficiency and effectiveness of the new product process to avoid wasteful expenditures of scarce resources.

Acceptance of popular myths concerning the new product development process discourages firms from taking less dramatic but more effective steps. The solution is to obtain in-depth understanding of market need prior to development, to focus on innovation instead of invention, and to use systematic and efficient procedures in all phases of the new product development process.

We have developed procedures which assure that the many facets of the process are given adequate attention and coordination. The concepts and procedures have been developed over the past 25 years in working with actual firms both large and small, serving industrial, consumer, and military markets.

Our first-hand experiences have shown that when the procedures described in subsequent chapters are followed, the chances of product success are greatly increased, as is the overall efficiency of the entire new product development process.

The philosophy and conceptual basis for the Bacon-Butler procedure are presented in Chapter 2, followed by a series of chapters explaining how the various concepts are made operational in the real-world environments of industrial firms.

Footnotes to Chapter 1

[1] Booz, Allen, and Hamilton, Inc., *Management of New Products* (New York, 1960).

[2] Charles W. Sherwin and Raymond S. Isenson, "Project Hindsight," *Science,* Vol. 156 (June 23, 1967), pp. 1571–77.

[3] Paul J. Marinaccio and Michael W. Dean, "Finite Element Analysis in Plastic Product Design," *Plastics Design Forum* (March/April, 1979), pp. 47–54.

[4] C. Freeman, et al. "Success and Failure in Industrial Innovation" [Project SAPPHO]. Centre for the Study of Industrial Innovation, The University of Sussex, England, 1972.

[5] David S. Hopkins and Earl L. Bailey, "New Product Pressures," *The Conference Board* (June 1971), pp. 16–24.

[6] James M. Utterback, "The Process of Technological Innovation," *Academy of Management Journal* (March 1971), pp. 75–88.

[7] Michael Michaelis and William D. Carey, *Barriers to Innovation in Industry: Opportunities for Public Policy Changes (Executive Summary).* Prepared for the National Science Foundation by Arthur D. Little, Inc., and the Industrial Research Institute, September 1973.

[8] Erik A. Haeffner, "The Innovation Process," *Technology Review* (March–April, 1973), pp. 18–25.

[9] Frank R. Bacon, Jr., H. W. Welch, Thomas W. Butler, Jr., Robert Hamilton, Robert Norman, and Wilson P. Tanner, *Methods for Evaluating Electronic Countermeasures in Ground Forces Applications,* Electronic Defense Group, The University of Michigan, Ann Arbor, December 1953 (S).

[10] Frank R. Bacon, Jr., Thomas W. Butler, Jr., and Wilson P. Tanner, *Tactical Use of Electronic Countermeasures,* Electronic Defense Group, The University of Michigan, Ann Arbor, July 1954 (S).

[11] Frank R. Bacon, Jr., *VT Fuse Countermeasures Systems Analysis,* Electronic Defense Group, The University of Michigan, Ann Arbor, April 1957 (S).

[12] Frank R. Bacon, Jr., and Richard H. Lewis, "Progress in the Development of Quantitative Market Requirements Models for Use in Long-Range Product Planning." Paper presented at the 7th International Meeting of the Institute of Management Sciences, New York, October 1960.

[13] Edward Ames, "Research, Invention, Development and Innovation," *The American Economic Review,* Vol. LI (June 1961), pp. 370–81.

[14] U.S. Department of Commerce, *Technological Innovation: Its Environment and Management* (Washington, D.C.: U.S. Government Printing Office, 1967), p. 2.

Chapter 2

Philosophy of Our Approach to
Successful Innovation

Given the complex and deeply rooted nature of the innovation problem, one would not expect the solution to be simple. The procedures we offer are a synthesis of techniques developed by ourselves and others. In this chapter we present an overview of the essential ingredients for successful innovation underlying the Bacon-Butler approach. In subsequent chapters we will detail the application of these ingredients.

Five ingredients believed essential for successful innovation are summarized in Figure 2.1. They represent an expansion of the three key elements presented in Chapter 1. To be successful in product innovation a firm (1) should shift to a marketing orientation; (2) should match its resources both qualitatively and quantitatively to new product opportunities; (3) should develop screening criteria which reflect its objectives and strengths; (4) should analyze market (user) need in sufficient depth (as well as other requirements for success) before technical developments; and (5) should organize, staff, and fund the new product development function properly for long-run success.

ESSENTIAL INGREDIENTS FOR
SUCCESSFUL INNOVATION

- Shift to marketing orientation.
- Choose opportunities which match resources.
- Develop proper screening criteria.
- Conduct requirements research in sufficient depth before technical development.
- Organize, staff, and fund adequately for long-run success.

Figure 2.1

1. Shifting to Marketing Orientation Places Focus on Meeting Customer Needs

Three general business orientations have been recognized in marketing literature for a number of years.[1] These include "production," "sales," and "marketing" orientations, as depicted in Figure 2.2.

American industry has been characterized as being largely *production*-oriented from the late 1700's through the early 20th century.[2] This was the period in our history of industrialization and economic development. Large unmet needs existed for goods, both consumer and industrial, leading businesses of that era to emphasize maximizing production (of largely existing products) to meet this large untapped demand of a growing new country.

The era of "production" orientations was followed (with some overlap in time) by a *"sales"* orientation. This era began about the first quarter of the 20th century in America and extended to

---

BUSINESS ORIENTATIONS

Production Orientation
Focuses On: What we can make
Deemphasizes: What we know how to sell
Ignores: Customer needs

Sales Orientation
Focuses On: Pushing what we've got
Deemphasizes: Meeting customer need through product innovation

Marketing Orientation
Focuses On: Meeting customer needs
Requires: (1) Precise definition of target markets
                     (2) Detailed understanding of customer needs
Results In: (1) All business functions oriented toward serving customers
                     (2) Above average long-run profit

Figure 2.2

about mid-century. During this period the earlier demand had attracted sufficient business developments for substantial competition to emerge in most classes of goods. The emphasis then shifted from maximizing production output to convincing customers to buy "our" product rather than that of competitors. Thus the term "sales" orientation. The focus here was to convince the customer that "our" (existing) product was superior to that of the competition, rather than to seek ways to better meet customer needs through product innovation.

Following the efforts to meet pent-up demands generated by scarcities during World War II, the limitations of the sales orientation become more apparent as firms struggled to compete in an environment of rapidly expanding and changing needs. The economic prosperity of the 1950's gave rise to needs for different products to meet requirements of various market segments. The quickening pace of technological development during World War II provided additional fuel for the movement toward increased product innovation.

Thus the *marketing* orientation emerged in the late 1950's and developed during the 1960's to its present-day concept. As shown in Figure 2.2, this business orientation focuses all the firm's activities on meeting customer needs (at a profit).

The implementation of the concept requires a precise definition of the target market (segments) to be served and a detailed understanding of the needs of the various segments. This knowledge allows the firm to develop products which better meet the needs of the segments served, thus providing more value to the user (than competing products). When the business is properly managed, all business functions become oriented toward serving customer needs and the greater value to the customer is translated into above average long-run profits to the firm.

From this brief sketch of the "marketing" orientation, it should be obvious that this business orientation is conceptually superior to it two predecessors, yet two decades after its inception, many firms have not been able to implement the concept. Why? Our experience leads us to the conclusion that the primary problem lies in the inability to define the target market segments and associated customer needs *with sufficient detail and precision* to make the concept operational. Our techniques are designed to overcome this deficiency and thus permit the concept to be more widely used. The techniques also involve two additional concepts closely related to the marketing orientation, the concept of a product, and of a marketing strategy.

Definition of a "Product"

Ask someone to define what they mean by the term, "product," and they will usually start describing the physical attributes of a device, material, or piece of equipment. To properly operationalize the "marketing" orientation (concept), a firm must understand its "product" as described in Figure 2.3. A firm's "product" is much more than a physical device, it is the summation of all need-satisfying elements, as shown in the figure. Of course, the physical product is usually of central importance, but other aspects may add up to provide equal or even greater value to the user. The package, instructions, warranty, installation, maintenance, spare parts, and availability all meet customer needs and thus contribute to the value of the total "product." This is true of many "install-it-yourself" consumer products such as radio-controlled garage door openers and window air conditioning units; and it is true of industrial products such as standard machine tools.

Additionally, customer needs (especially for consumer products) are met by identifying with the image projected by the product, which may be generated or enhanced by advertising and promotion. Examples include items which are "conspicuously con-

---

A PRODUCT

Is The Summation Of All Need-Satisfying Elements Which Include:

1. The Physical Product, and its many specific features, options.
2. The Package: to protect, handle, store, inform.
3. The Instruction Materials: How to assemble and use.
4. The Warranty.
5. The Installation, service, and spare parts availability.
6. The Place(s) where and when product is available for purchase.
7. The Promotion: information provided, image created.
8. The Price(s), with and without options, credit availability and terms.

Figure 2.3

20

sumed," such as autos, bicycles, skis, and clothing, as well as commercial products such as office copying machines. Xerox has devoted considerable resources to its TV ads which emphasize, "It's really a Xerox." And needs are met by terms of purchase, credit availability, and ability to buy at prices with and without options. This is true of most consumer durables such as washers and dryers, refrigerators, as well as computer systems for businesses.

Starting from scratch, to identify and totally define a new "product" is a complex undertaking. But to do so greatly enhances the development of the necessary marketing strategy.

Definition of Marketing Strategy

A marketing strategy, a second concept, closely related to the "marketing" orientation and the concept of a "product" described above, is illustrated in Figure 2.4. According to this definition, a marketing strategy for a new product (or product line) consists of 5 elements: (1) The definition of the target market (segments) and the specification of the (2) product (3) place (channels), (4) promotion, and (5) price elements.[3] As also shown in the figure, essential to the specification of each of these elements in the strategy is a detailed understanding of customer need in the market segments to be served. Therefore, when developing a new product,

---

A MARKETING STRATEGY FOR A
GIVEN PRODUCT LINE

Includes:
  1. Definition of the target market(s)
     —Definition of market segments (and basis for segmentation)
  2. Specification of the 4 P's
     —Product
     —Place
     —Promotion
     —Price

All Of Which Requires Detailed Understanding
Of Customer *NEED*

Figure 2.4

the proper analysis of customer needs aids immensely in specifying the entire marketing strategy to be later used for the product.

One can also see why a marketing orientation is vital to successful new product development. By understanding user needs in depth, "products" can be designed to meet target customer needs, and the proper marketing strategies for implementation can be developed.

For example, by better understanding the requirements for energy storage and flex properties for vaulting poles, AMF was able to utilize new analysis techniques and materials to design a pole with significantly greater "lift" characteristics. New world records, both indoors and out of doors, were established with this pole. (See Figure 2.5) Immediately thereafter no world-class vaulter would consider using any other.

In a similar way, greater in-depth understanding and analysis of requirements for gymnastic equipment led to the development of improved parallel bars, horizontal bars, balance beams, and even mats for floor exercises (see Figure 2.6). The changes in parallel bars have permitted gymnasts to perform routines never before possible. Improved materials in mats now permit gymnasts to practice for a much longer time without developing shin splints.

Furthermore, it was a series of modest improvements in each of the products which enabled this firm (AMF) to become a major factor in a market long dominated by others. Thus, as these examples show, profitable operations were almost completely assured from the beginning of product design to later commercialization. For these reasons, the use of the marketing orientation is one of the key elements in the Bacon-Butler approach to planned innovation.

2. Matching Resources to Opportunities Avoids Strategic Errors

The concept of proper matching of resources to opportunity originated out of experiences in developing long-range product strategy in the computer field in the mid-fifties, when that technology was in its infancy. A comprehensive analysis of the emerging market potential indicated that a smaller firm's resources would be severely strained and would likely be spread too thin if it attempted to serve all segments of the market in view of the much

Figure 2.5   Olympian Bob Seagren about to use the AMF Pacer III Vaulting Pole.

larger resource base of its chief competitor. The appropriate strategy was to concentrate resources in selected segments in order to better serve the needs there, despite the major competitor whose larger overall resources at that time were devoted to serving all market segments.

Figure 2.6   AMF American Balance Beam.

Since that early experience the concept has been further refined and made operational through working with many other
firms. The result is the present concept described below.

A Qualitative and Quantitative Match is Required

There are two aspects of the concept useful in providing
guidance to new product innovation. To be successful a firm
should achieve a *qualitative* and a *quantitative* match of resources to
the opportunity. This means the company should have or be able
to readily acquire the right kind of resources (technical, production, marketing, financial, management) and the right quantity
or size of resources (financial, manpower, production, marketing,
etc.) to serve the chosen market segment as well or better than
one's competition. The concept is further clarified by considering
two major mistakes commonly made.

Spreading Resources Too Thin

The first mistake is to spread resources too thin on opportunities which are too large or too complex (technically or managerially). This problem is often faced by small firms with a narrow technical, manufacturing, or marketing base. An attractive
opportunity exists for the company, but its resources are inadequate to the large task. If the company persists, it will be unsuccessful, because a competitor with a more suitable match of resources
(in kind and size) will be able to better meet the needs of the
market segment. For example, a number of firms, some quite
sizable, found in the early days of the computer field, that it was
not easy to be "another IBM," and eventually withdrew from the
market.

Wasting Resources on Inadequate Opportunities

The second error is to pursue opportunities which are too
small or too simple (again, technically or managerially). This is the
classic situation faced by large firms which develop new products
for markets which they later find are too small or represent an
uneconomical use of production or marketing resources. This was
the case with AMF's early entry into the robotry field through the

acquisition of Versatran. After entry the market did not expand as rapidly as many anticipated, and the division was sold because resources could be better used elsewhere. In such a situation the largest element of cost is the opportunity cost—the cost arising from lost time and resources which could have been devoted to a more suitable opportunity (in kind and size), with appropriate resulting profit.

Matching Resources Results in Leading From Strength

Using the concept of matching resources to opportunities does much more than help avoid mistakes. It leads, positively, to the selection of profitable opportunities when it is used together with an understanding of the firm's strengths and weaknesses. It insures that the firm will be utilizing its major strengths when undertaking new product innovations. Leading from strength is important in minimizing the risks of new product innovation. These ideas are incorporated in the principles for devising new product screening criteria explained in the following section.

3. Developing Proper Screening Criteria Assures Right Direction and Type of Growth

A good deal has been written on new product selection (screening) criteria.[4] Long lists of factors have been suggested, together with systems for weighing each factor and obtaining composite overall ratings.[5] Our experience in dealing with many firms using different screening and evaluation systems has led to the following general criteria for screening new product opportunities.

First, the screening process should be a direct reflection of company (or divisional) objectives, because new product innovations are a principal means for moving a firm toward its objectives.

Second, screening should reflect the qualitative and quantitative resources of the firm. One of the principal objectives of the screening process is to assure that new opportunities represent a good match for the resources of the company.

Third, the criteria used for screening should reflect the strengths and weaknesses of the firm. The screening process

26

should assure that the strengths of the firm will be effectively brought into play in new product innovations. Likewise, the screening criteria should guide the firm away from selecting opportunities where it has no strengths and no ability or desire to readily obtain them.

The risks are typically large enough in new product innovation, as shown earlier in Chapter 1, that selection of new products should be made to assure as much as possible that all the cards are stacked in favor of ultimate success, and are moving in the direction intended by company objectives.

4. Requirements Research Gives Direction to Technical and Market Developments

In Chapter 1 we explained that the real objective of new product development is *commercial success,* or successful innovation. Requirements research, therefore, must be adequate to guide the new product development toward this ultimate objective. We have devised the model shown in Figure 2.7 to repre-

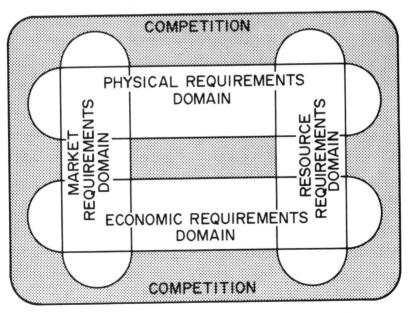

Figure 2.7   Total Requirements for Successful Innovation.

sent the total requirements for successful innovation. The total requirements are viewed as the simulaneous solution of multiple, overlapping requirements in five principal domains: (1) the marketing requirements domain, (2) the physical requirements domain, (3) the resources requirements domain, (4) the economic requirements domain, and (5) the competitive requirements domains.

As we shall elaborate in later chapters, the model guides our investigation of seven more detailed aspects of requirements listed in Figure 2.8.

The number one item in Figure 2.8 is an analysis of market need. This analysis focuses on the fundamental basis of the need, and seeks to determine the physical requirements of the product or service (item two in Figure 2.8) to meet the need, as well as the economic value of doing so. The research also examines the technical design requirements for the product, with special attention given to identifying feasible technical approaches which are within the resource constraints of the given firm.[6]

By identifying the physical and technical requirements for the product, it is possible to extend the analysis to include the technical, resource, and economic requirements for manufacture (item four in Figure 2.8). It is, of course, important that these requirements be within resource constraints as well.

The in-depth understanding of market need, economics of market value, production costs, and competitive offerings provide

---

REQUIREMENTS RESEARCH

Determines total requirements for successful innovation in sufficient depth to guide technical and market development including:
1. Market need.
2. Physical product requirements.
3. Technical design requirements.
4. Manufacturing requirements.
5. Marketing requirements.
6. Economic (cost and price) requirements.
7. Basis for competitive entry and protection from competitive reaction.

Figure 2.8

the basis for determining marketing and distribution requirements (items five and six in Figure 2.8). And lastly, no new product innovation can be successful without a sound basis for competitive entry and a subsequent basis for protection from competitive reaction. The anticipated basis for entry and protection should be identified and assessed *prior* to technical and market development.

Systematic Procedures Make Research Affordable

At this point, one may agree that research into each of the seven aspects is certainly desirable, but may ask, "How can any firm afford it for every new product?" The answer is that it is made possible and *affordable* by the research procedures we have devised and tested during the past two decades. The key is in knowing exactly what information is needed at each stage of the decision process and in using systematic and efficient procedures for obtaining it at each stage. We have spent many years learning what information is essential and in developing efficient procedures for obtaining it.

5. Organization, Staffing, and Funding Assure Proper Guidance, Coordination, and Support

There are several characteristics of new product innovation activities which must be given special consideration if innovation is to succeed within an ongoing business firm.

First, it must be recognized that most businesses are organized and their success measured by efficiency in the production and sale of existing products in the short run. The bottom line is short-run profit. New product innovation, an activity with pay-off in the medium to long run, is fundamentally disruptive of normal business activities and in conflict with management financial incentives. Thus, special organizational consideration and other management incentives are necessary if new products are to have a chance for success.

Second, successful new product innovation requires information, coordination, and support (manpower and budgetary) from diverse and often conflicting functional areas of interest: marketing, R & D, engineering, manufacturing, quality control (Q.C.), and finance. Yet success in new products requires that these diverse interests are combined in a climate of trust and mutual support. This places special requirements on the organization to facilitate the tremendous amount of lateral coordination required, and to build a cooperative atmosphere. It also places special requirements on the new product personnel—that they be able to understand all technical and marketing aspects of their activities, and be able to communicate with persons of diverse backgrounds, both within and outside the company.

Third, because new product activities are a principal means by which long-range growth objectives are implemented, these activities need continued guidance from top management. Organizationally, the function must be placed to receive such guidance. Specific recommendations regarding organization, staffing, funding, and operational procedures to assure successful coordination and control of new product innovations are included in a later chapter.

Summary

In order to solve the fundamental problems inherent in the new product innovation process, we have developed an approach consisting of five essential ingredients. First, a firm should shift to a marketing orientation, because this will focus attention on meeting customer needs. Second, firms should achieve a matching of resources to new product opportunities in order to avoid the strategic errors of spreading resources too thin on excessively large or complex opportunities, or wasting resources on inadequate ones. Third, a screening process should be developed which reflects the company objectives and its qualitative and quantitative resources, and enables the firm to lead from strengths in selecting new product opportunities to pursue.

Fourth, requirements research should be undertaken to give direction to technical and market developments prior to their initiation. All aspects of requirements for successful innovation must be investigated: market need, physical and technical product requirements, production and marketing requirements, as well as economic considerations of market value and costs and competition. Fifth, the new product activity must be organized, staffed, and funded to meet the special problems created by the disruptive nature of the activity, its inherent complexity, and the intensive need for coordination, and to assure guidance and support from top management.

The above five ingredients express our philosophy. We have developed, tested, and refined a number of procedures to implement this philosophy, which are contained in the remaining chapters.

Footnotes to Chapter 2

[1] See E. Jerome McCarthy, *Basic Marketing: A Managerial Approach,* 6th edition (Homewood, Ill.: Richard D. Irwin, Inc., 1978), pp. 27–30.

[2] *Ibid.*

[3] *Ibid.*

[4] For a good summary, see Patrick E. McGuire, *Evaluating New Product Proposals* (New York: The Conference Board, Inc., 1973), pp. 26–32.

[5] *Ibid.*

[6] For a brief description of other need assessment techniques, see Knut Holt, "Need Assessment in Product Innovation," *Research Management,* July 1976, pp. 24–28.

SECTION TWO

STRATEGIC PLANNING PROCEDURES

Chapter 3

Overview of Strategic Planning Procedures

Our procedures for implementing the concepts presented in the first two chapters are organized in two major sections. The present section (II) containing Chapters 3 through 7 deals with strategic considerations. This is followed by Section III, containing Chapters 8 through 14, dealing with steps for strategy implementation through new product innovation.

The relationships among the four chapters involved with strategic issues is shown in Figure 3.1.

Notice that there are three major inputs to the restatement of objectives (Chapter 5): (1) the analysis of strengths and weak-

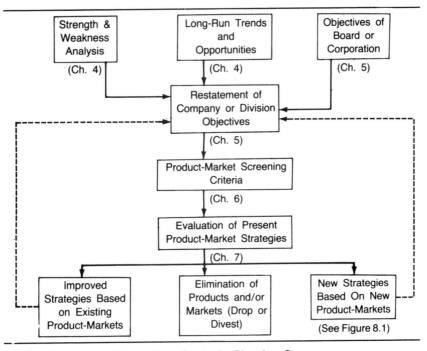

Figure 3.1 Strategic Planning Steps.

nesses (Chapter 4), (2) analysis of long-run trends and opportunities (also discussed in Chapter 4), and (3) the desires of the board of directors (or corporate objectives in case the unit under consideration is a division). Then, after these inputs have influenced the restatement of objectives, they flow through in greater detail (together with the restatement of objectives) to provide the basis of the product-market screening criteria (Chapter 6).

The product-market screening criteria are used first to evaluate existing product-market strategies (Chapter 7) and later to evaluate new product opportunities.

There are three outputs from the evaluation of present product-markets: (1) improved market strategies based on existing products (developed through changes in other variables: target market, price, promotion, or place), (2) elimination of products and/or markets, and (3) new market strategies based on new products. The dotted line leading from both activities back to objectives is to indicate that the total result of these activities should meet the objectives. New product innovation is, of course, concerned with the second of the two activities. However, both are vitally important in achieving objectives.

Changes in market strategies which do not involve new products usually entail less risk, time, and cost. Indeed, if short- and long-term objectives can be met merely by changing other variables (other than the product) in the marketing strategy, it is almost always preferable. But sooner or later, new products will be needed, as we have shown in Chapter 1. The place to start is with an assessment of strengths and weaknesses, to which we now turn.

Chapter 4

Identifying Strengths and Weaknesses and Long-Run Trends

"But above all, to thine ownself be true," is advice as applicable in the selection of new products opportunities today as it was in Shakespeare's day concerning human affairs. Our philosophy of successful new product innovation requires a matching of resources to opportunities and utilization of a firm's strengths. By leading from strength and "flowing with the stream" of long-run external trends a firm helps avoid taking unnecessary risk, thereby enhancing the probability of success.

As will be discussed in Chapter 5, a clear and unbiased understanding of a firm's strengths and weaknesses and a grasp of the nature of relevant long-term trends are necessary in framing objectives to guide the future direction of the company. But even beyond the statement of objectives, which can be rather general in nature, a good understanding of these elements is also essential to the statement of new product screening criteria, to be discussed in Chapter 6. As we shall explain there, the strength and weakness analysis provides the basis for the qualitative screening criteria. But what is a strength, and how is one identified?

A strength is a *unique combination* of capabilities or resources (technical know-how, special production equipment, marketing personnel, etc.) relative to competition which provides the basis for competitive advantage. An example of the definition of a specific capability is shown in Figure 4.1. This example, included with the permission of Donnelly Mirrors, Inc., shows how detailed the definition must be. An example of a unique combination of capabilities which results in a *strength* for the same firm is shown in Figure 4.2. Thus, different unique combinations of capabilities relative to competition result in different strengths.

Every firm has such unique combinations of capabilities, which make it different from every other firm. But perhaps not too surprisingly, as Shakespeare suggested was the case in human

"Good Glass-Handling Capability"

"State of the art production skills in cleaning, cutting, bending, and laminating medium- to high-volume quantities of standard float glass, standard sheet, and tempered glass in sizes of .5 to 5 square feet and thicknesses in the range of .1 to .5 inches."

Figure 4.1

affairs, in business affairs many participants are not fully cognizant of their own strengths and weaknesses. This we have found in helping top managers in many firms define their own firm's strengths and weaknesses. The objective of the strength and weakness analysis is thus to identify those strengths, so that the firm can then lead from them with its new product development activity, as summarized in Figure 4.3. Typically every firm can define three to six unique combinations of capabilities which provide different major strengths relative to competition in different product-markets. Procedures which facilitate the definition process are discussed below, following the discussion of trends.

EXAMPLE OF UNIQUE COMBINATION OF
CAPABILITIES = A STRENGTH

"Good Glass-Handling Capability"
  plus:

1. Reputation as proven reliable supplier to certain industry segments plus:

2. Certain specific research and engineering skills in specific technologies, plus:

3. Certain size of financial resources, plus:

4. Specialized production know-how or equipment, etc.

Figure 4.2

Figure 4.3

Long-Run Trend Analysis

The objective of long-run trend analysis is to identify those major forces which will have an impact on the firm or division within its strategic planning horizon (typically 5 to 10 years ahead). In making this analysis one cannot consider all trends in the world, but must focus on those which most likely will have a major impact on the particular firm or division within the time period in question. Otherwise, such an analysis is an impossible task, because many diverse trends will affect the firm to some degree.

It is helpful to make the trend analysis according to product-market or functional area along with the strength and weakness analysis. In Figure 4.4 we show a list of trend areas to be considered, with typical examples. It is important to note that trends may affect market opportunities (including the competition's) and all functional areas of the business (manufacturing methods, technologies, etc.).

Procedure for Defining Strengths and Weaknesses and Trends

A two-pronged approach has proven useful in stimulating the introspection necessary to define a company's strengths and weaknesses and relevant trends. The two approaches, outlined in Figure 4.5, involve evaluating major successes and failures in pro-

CHOOSE OPPORTUNITIES IN CONSONANCE
WITH LONG-RUN TRENDS

1. Technical
   - Rate of technical progress (advances in hand calculators)
   - New scientific discoveries (solar energy conversion)
   - New substitute technologies (micro circuits for watches)
   - New materials (structural plastics, coatings)
   - New processes and production methods (high-energy rate forming, numerical control)

2. Economic
   - Inflation, domestic and international
   - Changing costs of labor, material, capital, transportation, energy, taxes.
   - Changing income distribution—domestic and foreign
   - International value of the dollar

3. Social
   - Changing life-styles affecting marriage and family, dress, appearance, diet
   - Diminishing importance of work ethic
   - Growth of consumerism

4. Demographic
   - Changing population growth rate and age composition of: youth, young adults, senior citizens, white and non-white
   - Regional shift in population
   - Growth and decline in urban and suburban regions

5. Political
   - Growth in regulation and controls
   - Product liability
   - Environmental protection
   - Welfare support
   - Medical insurance
   - Military readiness
   - Foreign trade agreements

Figure 4.4

PROCEDURE FOR IDENTIFYING STRENGTHS
AND WEAKNESSES

1. Evaluate Product-Markets
   - Analyze outstanding successes and failures; why?
   - Seek explanatory patterns

2. Evaluate Functional Areas
   - Production
   - Research and Engineering
   - Marketing
   - General Management
   - Financial Resources

Figure 4.5

duct-markets and evaluating the major functional areas of the business.

Typically, the authors start with a meeting of the chief executive officer (CEO) or chief operating officer (COO), and the vice presidents (or managers) of each of the functional areas. The purpose and objective of the task is explained. Examples of capabilities and combinations of capabilities such as those shown in Figures 4.1 and 4.2 are presented and discussed. Individual managers are asked to make a preliminary evaluation of the strengths of his functional area (relative to typical competition) and trends affecting the area and be prepared for a later discussion with the same group. The CEO or COO and marketing executive typically undertake the analysis of major successes and failures by product-markets as discussed below. They also analyze major trends affecting market opportunities and competition.

**Evaluation of Product-Market Strengths and
Weaknesses and Trends**

This aspect of the analysis is best done by the top marketing executive in discussion with the most experienced and knowledgeable market managers and/or salesmen. If possible, the CEO or COO should participate in this evaluation to provide additional insight and balance for greater objectivity.

The identification of product-market strengths and weaknesses and trends is facilitated by first examining outstanding product successes and failures, leaving moderately successful products for later analysis—to be tackled after an explanatory pattern has been at least partially identified.

The purpose of the analysis is to identify which product or program attributes, including the associated marketing program, timing, etc., seem *largely* to account for the success or failure of the product in a specific market. Major trends affecting the continuing success of each product-market should also be identified.

The concept of a "product" has to be broadly construed for the analysis, as described earlier in Chapter 2. One must keep in mind that a product is not merely a physical collection of hardware, but the entire collection of "need-satisfaction" elements. Thus a service can be a "product." Furthermore, it is important to recognize that the same product may be seen differently by different markets. Success in one market may be due to one set of attributes while success (or failure) in another market may be due to different attributes. Therefore, it is very important to focus on product-market combinations when trying to explain success or failure.

The physical characteristics, cost, and performance of the product are, of course, centrally important in the analysis. However, other important elements include ability to develop and produce on schedule, availability of service and spares, ease of operation of test equipment, etc. An appropriate total list of need-satisfaction elements should be developed for each product-market. Each should be examined in light of the total list of elements to identify the major strengths and weaknesses.

After completing this exercise for the outstanding successful product-market, an attempt should be made to identify those primary strengths which these product-markets have *in common* and, it is hoped, which product-market failures lacked. The process should then be repeated for the outstanding product-market failures as well as for negative or adverse trends. The output from this analysis should be compared with the output of the similar analysis of strengths within functional areas, discussed below.

Evaluation of Strengths and Weakness
by Functional Areas

While the analysis of major successes and failures and trends related to product markets is being done, a parallel effort should be made to examine each functional area. The marketing executive has two tasks, the analysis of his own function, as well as the product-markets, as described above.

A successful procedure has been to ask each functional manager to first identify his unit's best capablity (relative to competition in typical markets served). After these have been identified, a similar review should be made of outstanding deficiencies (again relative to competition in typical markets served). In a similar way the manager should identify the major positive and negative trends affecting his functional area. In making these assessments the managers often involve or request the opinions of foremen or supervisors within their domain of responsibility.

The main objective of the analysis is to identify within each functional area the specific capabilities, talents, skills, and facilities which are the very best that unit has relative to the state of the art and the trends affecting the competitive continuance of these capabilities. For example, R&D may have a tuned-rotor gyro development group that is considered the best in the industry for certain market requirements. Engineering may have a special capability for computer-aided design which is likewise as good or better than any in the industry. Manufacturing may have a special capability of coordinating the subcontracting of assembly and checkout of complex systems, which provides a cost-competitive edge on contracts undertaken in certain market segments.

In identifying these capabilities it is important at first to be very specific, detailed, and narrow in the definitions. Later, specific capabilities can be combined if this is desirable.

The detailed specificity is important because some of these statements will be used later as product screening criteria. Looking back at the definition of "Good Glass-Handling Capability" shown in Figure 4.1, and the unique combination of capabilities shown in Figure 4.2, one can see that it would be relatively easy to determine whether a new opportunity will utilize the particular capability or the entire strength.

43

Combining the Results of Both Approaches

Having made independent appraisals of the product-markets and functions, the managers need to reassemble and compare notes. This session is usually very educational for those involved, because typically there is considerable disagreement about what constitutes the best capabilities and reasons for success or failure in product-markets. Of course, the more disagreement, the more important it is to go through the exercise. Disagreements are usually resolved by trying to identify one or two of the strongest capabilities in each functional area on which all can agree. Likewise an attempt should be made to reach a consensus regarding a minimum number of characteristics associated with success and failure in past product-markets.

Often one of the first tasks of newly-formed Technical Boards (See Appendix) is to review these internal evaluations of capabilities and trends, thus providing additional objectivity in the assessments.

Out of such discussion, which typically requires several days in total, should come a list of specific capabilities (typically 6 to 10) and combinations of those capabilities (typically 3 to 6) which represent the greatest competitive strengths of the firm or division relative to typical markets served. Also out of such discussion comes understanding on the part of key executives, of the reasons behind the objectives and new product selection criteria, to emerge later. By involving the key management personnel in the initial steps in the new product innovation process, the probability of their later cooperation and support is greatly enhanced.

Once strengths and weaknesses and trends have been defined, objectives can be framed, and new product screening criteria developed.

Summary

Having defined strength and shown how specific capabilities can combine to form a strength, we have outlined an approach to analyze a firm's strengths and weaknesses. Additionally we have suggested identifying those major forces which will have a major impact on the firm as a means of analyzing and forecasting relevant long-run trends. These trends may involve technical, economic, social, demographic, and political factors.

Strength and weakness analysis may involve investigation of significant product-market successes and failures; however, a parallel effort should involve examining the firm's functional areas. The results of both appraisals should subsequently be combined and consolidated. When these analyses have been performed, the next step, restating objectives, follows. It is discussed in Chapter 5.

Chapter 5

Restating Objectives

Statements of objectives of large corporations need to be general to encompass the diverse interests of their groups and divisions. If one were to examine several typical statements of corporate objectives, often included in annual reports, one might easily conclude that the statements are written more to impress stockholders than to provide guidance to others within the organization. In helping firms restate objectives, we have found that objectives often have not been drafted with the intent of providing useful guidance to those responsible for acquisitions and/or new product developments. Quite often it is presumed that more specific guidance will be given verbally on a day-to-day basis.

The result is either lack of a clear understanding of the desired direction on the part of key managers in the firm, or direction that tends to shift from week to week. Because new product innovation is typically a long-term process (typically 3 to 5 years from idea to market introduction), the organization needs "a steady hand on the tiller" providing the direction. It must be clear, at least to the top management team, where the firm is going and why. One way to facilitate this is to have a written statement of objectives and goals. The basic criteria for the statement of objectives at the corporate, group and divisional levels are shown in Figure 5.1. Note that both quantitative and qualitative criteria are needed. Objectives need to become more specific as they move down the hierarchy, with product line goals being quite explicit in order to guide development of needed product additions and modifications. Objectives at every level should reflect the firm's strengths and trends identified earlier (Chapter 4).

Quantitative Criteria

Quantitative criteria should specify the amount and/or rate of growth desired in sales over the appropriate planning horizon.

47

CRITERIA FOR OBJECTIVES

1. Quantitative Performance Criteria
   - Amount and/or rate of growth in sales
   - Return on investment or net assets employed

2. Qualitative Criteria
   - Nature of business (product fields) preferred
   - Constraints to be recognized

Figure 5.1

The horizon may be 3 to 5 years for a medium-sized manufacturer of components, or may be 10 to 25 years for resource-based firms such as mineral or coal-mining enterprises. In addition to growth in sales, there should be criteria for return on investment or assets employed. Both are usually stated on an after-tax basis.

Return on sales is also an often-used criterion. It is appropriate if the basic nature of the business is not expected to change radically over the planning horizon. However, the criteria can be very misleading when many different kinds of businesses are included in one corporation. In this case return on investment or net assets employed is likely to be a more reliable measure.

Other criteria are useful to supplement these basic ones. Many firms still prefer some form of minimum number of months' payback, in addition to the more sophisticated return on investment criterion.

Qualitative Criteria

In addition to the quantitative criteria, managers need additional qualitative guidance concerning the product-markets in which the firm wishes to be involved. At the corporate level of a large firm the statement of product-markets preferred will typically have to be quite broad and general. However, there may be a particular direction of business thrust (usually based on certain strengths) which can be explicitly stated. At the group level the statement can be narrowed; and it can be made even more specific for a division or small firm.

Constraints Need to be Specified

It is often easier and even more useful to specify any constraints that should be observed. As shown in Figure 5.2, the principal constraints to be identified involve product-markets and resources. For example, many firms producing products for industrial markets do not wish to manufacture or market consumer products. Some firms refuse to manufacture any products for military or government markets. Others desire to manufacture any product that can be marketed through established distribution channels.

Geographic restrictions are common constraints to be recognized in seeking new products. The constraint may be due to high costs of shipping, inability to service beyond a given distance, and lack of marketing capability (and no desire to develop it) in certain areas, such as international markets. If any such constraints exist, they should be reflected in the statement of objectives.

Often a key constraint involves the use of an existing resource, such as a production facility, specialized machinery, a group of highly qualified technical people, or an excellent marketing organization, as mentioned above. In almost every firm in which we have consulted, there have been several such constraints, often unknown to key management personnel involved in seeking new product opportunities.

IMPORTANT CONSTRAINTS TO IDENTIFY

1. Product-markets to be excluded
2. Geographic restrictions
3. Utilize key resources:
   - People
   - Plants
   - Facilities
4. Growth internally, externally, or both
5. Limits on funds

Figure 5.2

Internal Development and/or Acquisitions

It is common for small firms to insist that growth must come through internal development to the exclusion of acquisition simply because they do not have sufficient resources for acquisition. In larger firms, and in divisions of large firms, growth by both routes should be considered when appropriate. However, periods of high interest rates may render acquisition unattractive, even for the largest of firms. Under such conditions internal growth may be the only reasonable approach for them as well. The statement of objectives should indicate whether one route or the other, or both, is to be considered; and the statement should be reviewed periodically and revised depending on economic conditions.

Limits on Funds

Finally, limits on the size of acquisitions or limits on funds for internal developments must be made clear to those investigating new opportunities. Often this constraint is written directly into the screening criteria to be discussed later, rather than in the statement of objectives.

The set of quantitative and qualitative criteria for the statement of objectives presented above represents a basic, or minimum, set of criteria. Most firms have other statements as well, which are suited to the particular firm.

Objectives may also be framed for particular new ventures to be undertaken. The same criteria apply, and the statement can usually be very explicit concerning constraints. An example of objectives framed by the Instrument Division of Lear Siegler, Inc., which sought diversification from its primary military business, is shown later in Chapter 6 together with the associated screening criteria developed.

Summary

It must be clear, at least to the top management team, where the firm is going and why. We have suggested that a written statement of objectives be prepared, including both quantitative and qualitative criteria. Constraints, including geographic, financial, and growth restrictions, should also be identified. An appropriate restatement of objectives leads to the development of new product screening criteria, the subject of Chapter 6.

Chapter 6

Framing Product-Market Screening Criteria

The development of product-market screening criteria is an important means by which several concepts discussed in Chapter 2 are made operational. It is by careful design of the screening criteria that we assure: (1) that new product developments are in keeping with company division objectives; and (2) that only those opportunities are pursued which represent a good match of resources both qualitatively and quantitatively (and thereby that the company will be leading from strength when undertaking any new opportunity).

A good bit of homework must be done in order to properly design such screening criteria. As we have shown in the two previous chapters, the CEO or COO (in consultation with his top managers) usually must first define the company's or division's major strengths and weaknesses and then restate its objectives. Having done this, the CEO or COO (again in consultation with his top managers) is also the one who must decide on the content of the product-market screening criteria. Often the activities of stating objectives, identifying strengths, and framing screening criteria blend together so that the statement of screening criteria is the major document produced.

Screening criteria can be written in many forms,[1,2,3] but no matter how formulated, the statement should contain the elements shown in Figure 6.1. The screening criteria should reflect the division's or company's quantitative and qualitative objectives. Therefore the screening criteria should contain appropriate statements concerning sales and ROI requirements, type of business or products which are preferred, those which are to be excluded, and other constraints to be recognized.

Statements should also be included which reflect the strengths to be utilized, and the minimum and maximum size of opportunities which would be consistent with the size of resources available. The screening criteria should also indicate the usual basis for

53

PRODUCT-MARKET SCREENING CRITERIA

1. Implement divisional or company objectives to assure:
   - Sales growth
   - ROI or RONA
   - Finding preferred type of business or product
   - Awareness of constraints
2. Assure matching of resources and leading from strengths; avoid weaknesses in matching unique combination of capabilities and size to opportunities:
   - Identify unique capabilities
   - Specify:
     —Maximum size of total market
     —Minimum size of total market
     —Share of market preferred
3. Identify basis for competitive advantage
4. Seek compatibility with long-run trends and opportunities

Figure 6.1

competitive advantage to be expected. They should also assure that the new opportunities chosen are compatible with long-run trends and opportunities in the external environment, as discussed previously in Chapter 5.

A typical worksheet for such screening criteria is shown in Figure 6.2, using a "fill in the blanks" approach. Both quantitative

I. QUANTITATIVE CRITERIA:
   A. As a minimum, maintain these averages over long term:
      1. Return on assets employed after tax (to   %).
      2. Return on sales after tax (to   %).
   B. Achieve a manufacturing profit within (   ) years consistent with the Division's long-term goals stated in A-1 and A-2.

	5 Yrs. (Millions)	10 Yrs. (Millions)	% Growth 5-10 Yrs.
C. Expected sales of present business (without major new product-market strategies) (Real $):	$ _____	$ _____	$ _____
D. Sales objective for present business plus addition of new product-market strategies (Real $):			
1. Minimum:	$ _____	$ _____	$ _____
2. Optimum:	$ _____	$ _____	$ _____
3. Maximum:	$ _____	$ _____	$ _____

continued on p. 55

E. Annual sales volume (for a single product) (Real $):
   1. Minimum: $ _____ $ _____ $ _____
   2. Optimum: $ _____ $ _____ $ _____
   3. Maximum: $ _____ $ _____ $ _____

F. Market Share:
   1. Preferred: Achieve at least (%) relative to (#) of principal competitors.
   2. Minimum: Achieve one of the ( ) largest absolute market shares.

G. Total annual investment available for new product-market strategies over next 5 to 10 years.
   Minimum: _____   Expected: _____   Maximum: _____

H. Investment preferred per year (over 3–5 year period) for a single product-market strategy.
   1. Minimum: $ _____ to $ _____
   2. Optimum: $ _____ to $ _____
   3. Maximum: $ _____ to $ _____

II. QUALITATIVE CRITERIA:

A. Nature of Business
   1. Products for Markets:
      a. _____
      b. _____
      c. _____
   2. Product Characteristics:
      a. _____
      b. _____
      c. _____
   3. Product-Markets to be Excluded:
      a. Products for _____
      b. Products with a life cycle of less than ( ) years.
      c. Products with _____

B. Strengths to be Utilized in Product-Markets:
   1. The capability of _____
   2. Ability to _____
      a. _____
      b. _____
      c. _____
   3. Reputation for _____
   4. Prior knowledge of _____
   5. Experience in _____

C. Basis of Competitive Advantage:
   1. _____ investments in _____
   2. Identifiable form of competitive advantages such as:
      a. Patent Protection regarding _____
      b. Significant Technical Expertise in _____
      c. Unique Manufacturing Skills in _____
      d. Field Sales and Product Support regarding ____

D. Long-Run Trends and Opportunities:
   1. _____
   2. _____
   3. _____

Figure 6.2   Worksheet for Product-Market Screening Criteria.

and qualitative criteria are included. A few explanatory remarks will help interpret the use of the form.

Quantitative Screening Criteria

Starting with the Quantitative Criteria Items—I-A-(1) and I-A-(2) in Figure 6.2—are typical measures of return on assets and sales, usually based on after-tax figures. Item I-B is one form of a break-even statement. Criteria I-C and I-D are used together to state the quantitative sales growth desired. Item I-C is a statement of the level of sales to be expected in five and ten years without major new product innovations. Often the sales are projected including product modifications, but with no new additions to existing lines. This projection (I-C) provides a benchmark for the sales objectives stated in I-D.

The minimum, optimum, and maximum sales levels for existing product-markets plus the addition of new product-markets is shown in I-D for five- and ten-year periods. Thus the difference between I-C and I-D represents the sales volumes in new products needed over the periods shown. Also calculated in I-C and I-D are the growth percentages over the five- to ten-year periods represented by the numbers inserted. This is used as a check on the practicality of attaining the sales amounts inserted. Quite often managers are used to thinking in terms of growth percentages rather than absolute dollar amounts. Each provides a check on the other.

Quantitative criterion I-E represents an attempt to state the limits of the optimum match of resources for a single product-market. The maximum level is the largest amount which the firm or division can reasonably handle without spreading itself too thin. For a single product-market, the minimum amount is perhaps the critical figure, because of the danger of the firm's wasting its resources on an inadequate opportunity, as was explained in Chapter 2.

The problem of spreading resources too thin on large opportunities is usually less severe because it can often be solved by focusing on narrower market segments. This is not always true, however, because some markets, such as hardware and maintenance supplies, require that a full line of product be carried in order to be competitive. It may be necessary to be fully committed or not at all.

Criteria I-F-(1) and (2) are expressions of share of market preferred. Following the recent work of the Boston Consulting Group and PIMS, indicating the importance of dominant market shares, many firms look only for opportunities where a significant share can be attained.[4]

Criterion I-G is a benchmark statement similar to I-C. It is an estimate of the minimum and maximum expected amounts of annual investment which the firm can devote to new product innovation over the planning period. It is inserted as a check on the reasonableness of (1) obtaining the amount of new product sales for the amount to be invested in development, and (2) as an upper limit on the sum of preferred investments per product per year as shown in I-H.

Criterion I-H indicates the minimum, optimum, and maximum investments preferred for development of a single product-market over a normal development cycle, typically three to five years. This is again a statement of the optimum matching of the firm's technical resources to opportunities. The maximum is perhaps the key criterion if the firm is to avoid projects which strain limited technical resources. A minimum investment criterion is useful as a check. Based on previous experience, a firm can usually estimate the minimum investment likely to be required to produce the minimum sales for a single product in I-D.

Qualitative Screening Criteria

The worksheet for qualitative screening criteria shown in Figure 6.2 is perhaps more self-explanatory than that for the quantitative criteria. Criterion II-A-1 is a statement of the product-markets such as flight control equipment for commercial aviation, or residential and/or commercial electric lighting fixtures, etc., to receive primary (or exclusive) consideration based on the firm's objectives. Criterion II-A-2 is a statement of the characteristics of the product-markets which reflect the technical, engineering, or production strengths of the firm, based on the strength and weakness analysis. Examples of typical useful characteristics are such things as requirements for specially designed software, or microprocessor design, or ability to hold machined tolerances to $\pm$ .0001 inch or less, or ability to manufacture custom-designed micro-miniature components, etc., for specific market segments.

Product fields to be excluded (Item II-A-(3)) should include all classes of products or markets which are clearly beyond the objectives of the firm. Reasons for certain exclusions may be lack of technical capability, manufacturing skill, or marketing or managerial knowledge. For example, managers of firms serving industrial markets often believe that the firm does not have the capability or knowledge to enter consumer markets. Often managers of small or medium-sized firms have personal biases against certain types of products, for example, products for government or military markets. Whatever the reasons, all exclusions should be included to avoid wasting time on products certain to be rejected later.

Strengths to be utilized in new product-markets (Item II-B) represent the major capabilities which resulted from the strength and weakness analysis by function or department. They may include such capabilities as computer-assisted finite element analysis of structures, the ability to manufacture special electronic chips, the ability to provide technical service worldwide, etc. The basis for competitive advantage (Item II-C) is closely related to the previous item. The difference is that here the traditional bases of protection from competitive reaction are highlighted. These may include large investments in research on specialized manufacturing facilities, strong patent positions, or dominant market positions. Again the statements should be made as specific as possible, e.g., the analyst should designate exactly what facility or expertise or patent has provided the competitive advantage.

Long-run trends and opportunities (Item II-D) represent the major factors which are likely to affect the firm or division within the planning horizon. The trends may be positive: e.g., an increasing number of senior citizens creating or supporting market opportunities in health care; there also may be negative trends: e.g., declining birth rates leading to diminishing markets for baby apparel and food. Major relevant trends should be listed without attempting to state whether they are positive or negative. As new product-market ideas are screened, they should be examined to ascertain that the new business will flow with important trends and, especially, will not be going against any significant ones.

Weighting of Criteria

Additional criteria may be appropriate, as well. One should be aware, however, that generally the longer the list of criteria, the more restrictive the set of criteria becomes. Some form of weighting of criteria then becomes needed. A compromise technique, which has been successfully used by firms with whom we have consulted, is the use of a small set of absolutely essential criteria, together with a larger set of "desirable but not absolutely essential" criteria. The worksheet shown in Figure 6.2 has been used successfully in both ways: (1) without distinguishing essential and desirable criteria, and (2) with the first one or two items in each section considered "essential" and the remaining ones "desirable."

The question remains largely unanswered whether there should be further quantification of the importance to be attached to each factor in the screening criteria. A number of systems for doing so have been published.[2,3] Our experience has been that additional quantification beyond the two classes, essential and desirable, aids the decision process very little. At this stage of evaluation, information is usually sketchy, and often quite subjective. There is a danger of being misled by "over-quantifying" without adequate basis. By basing the screening decision on a few well-founded concepts—whether the opportunity leads in the direction desired, whether it is a good match for resources, and whether it would utilize strengths—one can quickly sort out those that make economic sense for the firm from those that don't.

A Useful Analogy

The choice of a new product-market by a firm is much like a person's choice of a mate. In the first place, it is a very personal thing. The choice reflects the particular needs of the firm, or person, at a given time. Secondly, the choice must be a two-way proposition—there must be a reasonably good match for success. Thirdly, a firm approaches the new product search with a set of general criteria. Nevertheless, when the right product opportunity comes along, it need not fit every criterion exactly. Other features are often so attractive that they transcend certain original criteria or make up for other deficiencies. Finally, the process is always exciting, because, ultimately, success will depend on resolving the many unexpected problems which no initial selection procedure can foresee. The most, then, that can be expected of the screening procedure is its ability to ascertain that the basic ingredients exist for a good match that leads toward the desired objectives.

Passing the Screen Is the Beginning, Not the End of Analysis

Passing the screen does not automatically mean that the product will be developed. Indeed not. Passing the screen only qualifies the new product-market idea for consideration at the next stage in the evaluation process. If a number of new product-market ideas have passed the screen, an executive decision must be made concerning the priorities for which the ideas will be evaluated. This decision is often made based on the status of existing product-markets and the sense of urgency felt in bolstering present product lines or providing needed diversification. Almost always the decision regarding priorities has a large degree of subjectivity and should be made by the chief executive with the advice of his top managers.

An Example

An example of a statement of objectives and associated new product screening criteria is shown in the series of Figures 6.3, 6.4, and 6.5 shown below. These statements were used to guide the efforts of a new venture group established in 1972 by the Instrument Division of Lear Siegler, Inc. The Division, a large manufacturer of aerospace products (Figure 6.3) sought to utilize its technological strengths to develop products for other markets. The objectives (Figure 6.4) and screening criteria (Figure 6.5) led to the successful development and introduction of the "Mail-mobile^R" system in 1976.[5]

Summary

The criteria and a basic worksheet procedure have been discussed for screening new product-market ideas or opportunities.

Who Are We?
A manufacturer of aerospace products for the military and commercial markets of the world . . .

Product Lines
- Digital Computers
- Navigation Systems
- Weapon Delivery Systems
- Guidance and Control Systems
- Ground Support Equipment

- Gyro Products
- Reference Systems
- Flight Displays
- Air Data Displays

Source: Lear Siegler Inc., Instrument Division, Grand Rapids, Michigan (included with permission).

Figure 6.3

These have been designed to provide merely an initial screening which can be done with minimal effort. Such criteria for specific firms should be prepared in written form and then circulated among key employees to help direct their thinking toward the types of opportunities needed by the company. One must be cautioned, however, to recognize that the mere existence of suitable procedures and criteria for selection does not guarantee success in application.

NEW VENTURE OBJECTIVES . . .

- Lessen our dependence on military business
- Utilize Division technological strengths
- Utilize the human and physical plant resources available in Grand Rapids
- Break even within three years
- Provide a profit margin which exceeds the margins from present miltary business

Source: Lear Siegler Inc., Instrument Division, Grand Rapids, Michigan (included with permission).

Figure 6.4

1. *Size of Market Opportunity*
   - The new product opportunity must be large enough to justify the Division's interest but yet not too large for LSI to handle with the resources available.
   - For any new product venture, the total market, expressed in sales potential in five years, should be a minimum of about $15 million per year.
   - The total sales which LSI reasonably can expect to capture should be large enough for LSI to be a major factor in the marketplace.
   - For any new product opportunity, the five-year sales potential for LSI should be a minimum of $7.5 million per year.
2. *Nature of the Opportunity*
   - The opportunity must be suitable to receive a major benefit from the Division's technological strengths.
   - The technological benefits may be found in any of the following:
     - A. A high-technology product in an advanced field.
     - B. Application of high technology to a field where the present technology is less sophisticated than LSI's present capability.
     - C. The technological benefit may be realized either in engineering the product or manufacturing a new product.
   - It is our hypothesis that it would be unlikely that any new venture would really benefit from the technological strengths of the Division unless there is a reasonably high degree of technical sophistication required in the design or production of the new product.
   - It is not our intention (with any new product venture) to utilize only the financial, managerial, and physical plant resources of the division. Thus, an opportunity to manufacture a low-technology product, using available plant space and financial resources, would not meet our new product venture criteria.
   - To meet our objectives, new product opportunities must be found in nonmilitary markets. The most likely candidates are in the industrial and commercial markets.
3. *Nature of Marketing:*
   - The new product opportunity should not require the development of a national distribution system for consumer products marketed to the consumer.
   - Market characteristics should yield typical order sizes of $5,000 or more.(The order could cover either one large item or a large OEM order or smaller dollar items.)

continued on p. 63

4. *Nature of Competition:*
   - The product opportunity should permit entry into a marketplace in order to obtain a large percentage of the total market potential.
   - The present competition will probably be small; but if it is not small, then the market should not be of major interest to the large firms in the field.
5. *Nature of the Market:*
   - The new product opportunity will most likely be in the very early stages of development.
   - The opportunity will most likely represent long-range growth trends which are more rapid than total economy trends.
   - The market may be so new and untapped that creative market development will be required.
   - Such a market should be reinforced by more than one of the following basic economic trends:
     - —Technological
     - —Demographic
     - —Social
     - —Economic.

Source: Lear Siegler Inc., Instrument Division, Grand Rapids, Michigan (included with permission).

Figure 6.5

Once a new idea passes the screen, much additional evaluative work remains before a decision is made to develop the new product. In the following chapters we will discuss how to insure the flow of new product ideas, and examine the series of procedures needed to evaluate them once they have passed the initial screening criteria.

Footnotes to Chapter 6

[1]McGuire, Patrick E., *Evaluating New Product Proposals* (New York: The Conference Board, Inc., 1973), pp. 26–32.

[2]John S. Harris, "New Product Profile Chart," *Chemical and Engineering News* (April 16, 1961), pp. 115–18.

[3]John T. O'Meara, Jr., "Selecting Profitable Products," *Harvard Business Review*, Vol. 39, No. 1 (January-February, 1961), pp. 83–89.

[4]Roger A. Kerin and Robert A. Peterson, "Analytical Techniques for Strategic Marketing Management: PIMS and Boston Consulting Group Perspectives," *Perspectives on Strategic Marketing Management* (Boston: Allyn and Bacon, Inc., 1980), pp. 11–18.

[5]See John G. Anderson, "Citibank Saves $150,000 in One Year and Improves Mail Delivery Service with Six Self-Propelled Vehicles," *Corporate Systems*, Vol. 2, No. 1, Feb./Mar. 1977, pp. 43–48. See also: "Mail-mobile: Office Automation's Last Link," *Government Executive*, Vol. 7, No. 6 (June 1977); and Robert S. Greenberger, "New Civil Servants Sound Off a Lot But Stay in Line," *The Wall Street Journal*, April 16, 1979, p. 1.

Chapter 7

Evaluating Present Product-Market Strategies For Growth Opportunities

After restating objectives, analyzing strengths and weaknesses and market trends, and having framed screening criteria, a firm has laid most of the groundwork to consider new product opportunities. But before proceeding to new products, every firm should assess (or reassess) how much growth and change is possible from present product-market strategies; i.e., to what extent objectives can be met by changes in market strategies which do not involve new products, as we explained earlier in Chapter 3 with reference to Figure 3.1. Our experience has shown that every corporation must seek profitable growth. It cannot stand still—it must change or die.

If sales and profit objectives can be reached by improved promotion, pricing, or distribution, these are likely lower-risk alternatives to investment in new products. However, if shortfalls are still anticipated in sales and profits from existing product-market strategies after such evaluation, new product-market strategies are called for.

In many firms the evaluation procedures we suggest in this chapter are performed periodically and do not need additional attention. If this is the case, the reader should proceed on to Chapter 8. If it is not the case, or you would like to review the procedures involved in this activity, then read on.

Again, it is useful to define the amount of change needed in both quantitative and qualitative terms. Management needs to know quantitatively how much increase in sales and profits will be needed over the planning period to meet the stated objectives. And management also must determine what type of change in the product offering, if any, is appropriate in order to produce the desired quantitative result in sales and profits.

Because there is a variety of well-known procedures in use today for analyzing both types of change, we need not give exhaustive treatment to the subject here. Instead, we will briefly describe selected techniques which apply to both types of change as well as procedures we have developed to help determine the type of qualitative change needed.

Determining Quantitative Amount of Change Needed

The quantitative amount of product change needed in any firm simply depends on the difference between the growth and profit objectives of the firm and the anticipated future sales and profit performance of existing products.

Under normal circumstances a firm is well aware of both of these aspects of its business. Not infrequently, however, a significant change in the business environment (such as loss of a major market, change in company ownership, or rapid technological change) will generate a need for reassessment of the firm's anticipated product performance.

A schematic outline of a procedure for analyzing the quantitative change needed in existing products is shown in Figure 7.1. The basic information needed (shown in the numbered sections of the figure) includes: (1) an analysis of sales and costs by existing product lines, and (2) an analysis of trends in the firm's basic product fields (economic, technological, and competitive). It is elemental that a firm cannot have profitable growth unless the product's selling price is greater than the product's costs. Yet many firms do not know the manufacturing and distribution costs by product line or by markets served.

Information from (1) and (2) is then used to prepare a forecast (3) of expected future sales and profits (product line profitability) from existing products.

The forecast (3) can be compared with the sales and profit objectives (4) to determine the amount of change (increase) needed in sales and profits to reach the corporate objectives. The change in sales and profits must then come from specific changes in current operations or in additions in the product offerings.

66

Profit Line Profitability Analysis

The analysis of existing sales and product line costs needed for the quantitative evaluation also contributes to determining the qualitative type of change needed.[1,2] Such analysis usually includes the information shown in Figure 7.2. Often this information is obtained routinely by the marketing and cost accounting organizations. Not infrequently, however, we have found this information unavailable, and considerable time and effort are re-

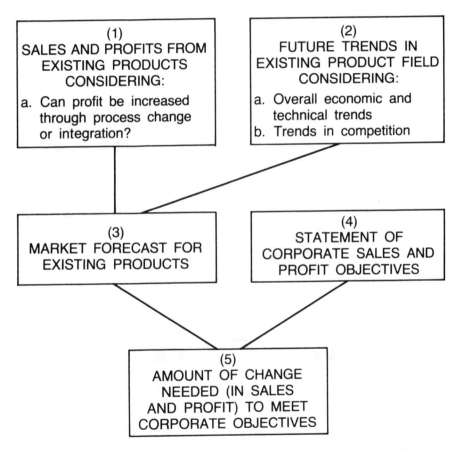

Figure 7.1 Procedure for Analyzing Total Amount of Product-Market Change Needed.

1. Amount of sales and costs (and profit contribution)
   a. by product
   b. by market or industry

2. Amount of sales and costs (profit contributions)
   a. by customer
   b. by type of customer
   c. by location of customers (and profit contribution)

3. Amount of sales and costs by type of application

4. Amount of sales and costs by type of distribution channel (if several are used)

5. Percentage of total market (market share) by
   a. type of product
   b. type of customer
   c. industry or other appropriate market segments

Figure 7.2

quired to generate an adequate base of knowledge before any meaningful product planning can be undertaken.

Product Life Cycle Analysis

In addition to sales analysis, another valuable and widely used technique for making product and marketing decisions is product life cycle analysis. Life cycle analysis attempts to identify which of four or five stages (introduction, growth, maturity, decline, and obsolescence) represent the current status of each product or product line. Once the stage is identified, the associated body of knowledge is applied to explain the present and expected product performance, and help determine appropriate changes in the product/marketing strategy, including pricing, advertising, and product variations.[3]

For example, a new product in the introduction stage would not be expected to be profitable; but one in the growth stage

68

should be reaching its maximum profit, while a product in the mature stage would be expected to produce a reduced profit (due to increased competition). A product entering the declining stage would be expected to produce lower profits, whereas a product in the obsolescence stage often produces moderate profits again, because few suppliers remain and a relatively good price can be obtained for a basic (stripped down) product.

Product life cycle analysis is useful in indicating whether sales and profits from existing products can be improved merely by changes in marketing, in production processes, or in the degree of integration in manufacture. For example, profits from a product in the mature stage of its life cycle (automatic dishwashers) about to enter the declining stages might be increased through cost-reducing redesign efforts, possibly guided by value engineering analysis.

In addition, value engineering analysis should also reflect any new technical developments such as the availability of new materials and/or new manufacturing techniques, which may affect production costs in the reasonable future.

Thus, product life cycle analysis used in conjunction with sales analysis aids in preparation of projections of sales and profits. It also provides insights into the nature of changes in product, marketing, or production which are appropriate to sustain sales and profit levels.

Trend Analysis

A meaningful market forecast is not made only on the basis of sales analysis, supplemented by product life cycle analysis. As shown in Figure 7.1 (and earlier in Figure 3.1), a second major input is needed for the preparation of market forecasts, namely, information on future trends which are likely to influence the firm's business.

Although the importance of various trends depends on the particular industry, the typical factors which deserve consideration in the preparation of market forecasts were shown previously in Figure 4.4. These are the same factors which already would have been considered in framing corporate objectives, as discussed in Chapter 5.

In preparing market forecasts, the same basic factors must be considered, but certain ones are examined in greater detail as they apply to specific products. For example, a manufacturer of medical equipment will closely monitor political developments regarding product liability and medical insurance, as well as the potential availability of certain new technologies and materials.

The techniques used to monitor and evaluate trends in these factors vary considerably depending on the size of firm, breadth of product offerings, and product fields of interest.[4,5,6,7,8,9] For example, most firms subscribe to a number of periodicals and specialized newsletter services, journals, and government publications which report on various factors such as pending legislation, economic trends, and technical developments in various fields. Many large firms, especially those doing business with the government, establish offices in Washington for continued liaison and reporting on forthcoming developments.

The Technical Board

A relatively inexpensive technique which can provide excellent monitoring of a wide range of technical developments is called the Technical Board. This concept, pioneered by us and now used by a number of firms, employs a group of outside technical advisors to broaden and deepen the technological outlook of the company.[5] The technical board is especially useful when used in conjunction with other techniques for technological forecasting such as relevancy trees, Delphi technique, scenario development, and technological progress functions.[6,7] A description of the composition and function of technical boards is included in the Appendix. It should be pointed out that the concept of an outside board of technical advisors could be easily extended to monitor trends in other functional areas as well, such as marketing or production.

Portfolio Analysis

During the years since we published our first edition of *Planned Innovation*, in 1973, considerable attention has been given by others to the development of techniques for evaluating existing business units and product lines. General Electric, an early leader in recognizing and implementing the "marketing orienta-

70

tion," developed the "Strategic Planning Grid" for evaluating existing and potential business opportunities.[10] (See Figure 7.3.) This procedure classifies existing and potential opportunities on a three-by-three grid according to *Business Strength* (high, medium, and low) and *Industry Attractiveness* (high, medium, and low). The object is to know which business deserves further investment, which would be maintained at status quo, and which phased out.

The Strategic Planning Institute of Cambridge, Massachusetts, an offshoot of the activity at GE, has developed an extensive computer-assisted model labeled "PIMS" (Profit Impact of Market Strategies) for evaluating existing businesses.[11] The Boston Consulting Group has also developed an evaluation procedure somewhat similar to the GE Strategic Planning Grid which classifies businesses within a two by two matrix according to industry growth rate and market share. (See Figure 7.4.) They have coined the well-known terms, "stars," "cash cows," "question marks," and "dogs" to signify respectively whether to continue investing, "milk" the existing investment, wait and see, or disinvest. Of course, this brief description does not do justice to the detailed considerations involved in any of the systems mentioned, but it does show the thrust of the efforts in evaluating existing and potential businesses for strategic planning purposes.

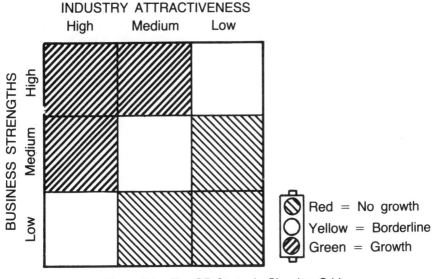

Figure 7.3 The GE Strategic Planning Grid

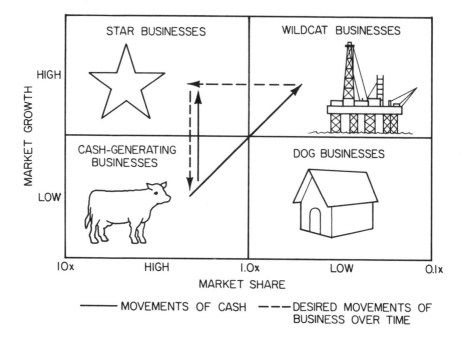

MARKET GROWTH

HIGH

LOW

STAR BUSINESSES

WILDCAT BUSINESSES

CASH-GENERATING
BUSINESSES

DOG BUSINESSES

10x   HIGH   1.0x   LOW   0.1x

MARKET SHARE

——— MOVEMENTS OF CASH ——— DESIRED MOVEMENTS OF
BUSINESS OVER TIME

Figure 7.4 Boston Consulting Group Grid.

Almost every firm with which we have interfaced uses these or somewhat similar procedures for the general type of guidance intended.[12,13,14] Our procedures overlap to a minor degree and are designed to go on to provide more specific guidance concerning the type of product changes or additions required to implement strategic growth plans.

Output From Analyses

Let us return now to the purpose of the sales forecast, which is based on the sales and trend analyses. As shown earlier in Figure 7.1, the amount of sales, profits, and percent return on assets (ROA) forecast from existing products is compared with company objectives to determine the quantitative amount of change needed to meet objectives. Often the output of such an analysis is shown for a number of years into the future as illustrated in Table 7-1. The example shown is for a medium-sized firm which has three product lines. The sales and profit forecasts for each product are

TABLE 7-1

TYPICAL OUTPUT FROM ANALYSIS OF TOTAL AMOUNT OF PRODUCT CHANGE NEEDED

Sales, Profit, and ROA Forecasts for
Existing Product-Market Strategies
(In Millions of Dollars)

	In 1 Year			In 3 Years			In 5 Years		
	Sales	Profit	ROA (%)	Sales	Profit	ROA (%)	Sales	Profit	ROA (%)
1. Product Line A	5.0	0.5	15%	5.2	0.5	14%	5.5	0.5	14%
2. Product Line B	7.0	0.3	8%	7.5	0.5	13%	8.0	0.6	13%
3. Product Line C	10.0	1.0	16%	10.5	1.1	16%	12.0	1.2	17%
4. Total	22.0	1.8	14%	23.2	2.1	15%	25.5	2.3	15%
5. Corporate objective	23.0	2.3	17%	26.0	2.6	18%	30.0	3.0	19%
6. Quantitative amount of change needed (line 5 – line 4)	1.0	0.5	3%	2.8	0.5	3%	4.5	0.7	4%

shown for three time periods—one, three, and five years—into the future.

The sales and profits for each product are totaled for each year (line 4) and compared with the corporate sales, profit, and % ROA objectives (line 5). The difference indicates the amount of additional sales, profits, and % ROA which must be generated through program changes or most likely through changes in product offerings. The quantitative difference for each time period indicates the extent and timing required of new product additions.

Determining Type of Change Needed

After determining quantitatively the amount of change needed in sales and profits, the more difficult question must be answered, "What type of qualitative product changes are needed and are appropriate to reach the quantitative objectives?"

Deciding what type of change is appropriate often is not an easy task. The task usually requires much "soul searching" and reevaluation of favorite product lines—long considered "old friends" of the company—which may have become marginally profitable and must be replaced. Product life cycle analysis and the other procedures can usually provide some guidance, as mentioned above. But more is often needed.[15]

Building on the previously framed statement of company objectives, and on an analysis of trends in the market environment for various company products and the firm's strengths and weaknesses, our procedure provides a means of classifying the type of change in each product or product line consistent with the company's product-market screening criteria.

Each product is examined and classified according to which of the following four degrees of change are most appropriate: (a) eliminating an existing product and replacing it with a new product for a new market; (b) adding a new product and/or marketing mix for the present market; (c) modifying the existing product for the present market; or (d) making no change in the existing product design, but improving the marketing mix.

The four types of product change range from the greatest change possible to the least possible. The greatest change possible is to add a new product line for a new market. (Hewlett Packard's or Texas Instruments' first entry into the scientific pocket calculator field.) This is essentially complete diversification from the present product and market. The second, and lesser degree of change, is to introduce a new product line to a present market. (Subsequent introduction of business pocket calculators.) The third, and still smaller type of change, is to modify present products or other elements of the marketing mix to better suit present markets. (Introduction of new models of scientific and business calculators sold through bookstores.) The fourth, and least, change is to make no change in the product, but to improve the marketing mix of existing products in the present market. (Reduction in price with additional distribution of calculators through discount stores.)

ALSO

NEW MARKETS

SAME PRODUCTS

Other, more finely divided classes of change can be defined (such as introducing a present product in a new market), but our experience with an expanded model has shown that the four types of change included are adequate for providing meaningful direction in most situations.[16]

Analysis Procedure

A three-step analysis procedure is used to evaluate the situation facing each product. The analysis begins with a broad scope of the market and product class, and the scope of both is narrowed at each successive step. The analysis focuses on market trends *relative* to company product-market screening criteria.

Step 1
a. Analyze the trend in the total industry market for the general type of product offered by the firm.
b. Compare the trend with corporate or divisional screening criteria: classify as relatively favorable or unfavorable. If favorable, proceed to step 2; if not, stop.

Step 2
a. Analyze the trend in the submarket(s) served by the firm for the specific type of product offered.
b. Compare the trend with corporate or divisional screening criteria: classify as relatively favorable or unfavorable; if favorable, proceed to step 3; if not, stop.

Step 3

a. Analyze the trend in performance of the firm's products in the submarket(s).

b. Compare the trend with corporate or divisional screening criteria: classify as relatively favorable or unfavorable.

As the steps indicate, the analysis proceeds from step to step until an *unfavorable* relative comparison (judgment) is made. At this step the analysis stops, and the appropriate type of change is indicated from among the four types previously listed. The framework for determining the appropriate selections at each step of the analysis procedure is shown in Figure 7.5.

The four possible outcomes (labeled situations 1, 2, 3, and 4) from the three-step procedure described above are shown in the figure. The four situations, listed in rows in the figure, are matched to the four types of product change, shown in the right-hand column, one of which is appropriate for each situation.

Illustration of Procedure

Let us illustrate the procedure by an application to the automotive rearview mirror example cited earlier. To apply the three-step analysis procedure the firm must decide on the appropriate product field and market definitions for its own business. In the example mentioned, the firm might have defined its product field as rearview mirrors for all purposes, such as: vehicular mirrors (including trucks, etc.), automotive mirrors, automotive rearview mirrors, automotive rear-vision systems, or automotive proximity warning devices.

The firm may have defined its total market as worldwide original equipment manufacturers of motor vehicles (or of autos alone), or as U.S. automakers alone. These are choices which the management must make initially, based on how it views the scope of its business.

For purposes of illustration, however, let us assume that the product-market definition for step 1 is chosen to be automotive rear-vision systems, and the total market of interest is worldwide motor vehicle original equipment manufacturers.

Proceeding then to step 2, the firm must define the submarkets and specific products offered to these markets. Let us assume that the submarkets of concern are U.S. and European

FRAMEWORK FOR SELECTING TYPE OF CHANGE NEEDED IN EXISTING PRODUCT-MARKET STRATEGIES

	Step (1)	Step (2)	Step (3)	Strategy Indicated
	Trend in Total Industry Market for the General Type of Product Offered	Trend in Submarket Served by the Firm for Specific Type of Product Offered	Trend in Performance of Firm's Actual Products in the Submarket(s) Served	Type of Change Needed
	(Each Relative to Product-Market Screening Criteria)			
SITUATION #1	UNFAVORABLE			(a) Elimination Strategy; Replace with New Product for New Market
SITUATION #2	Favorable	UNFAVORABLE		(b) Add New Product for Present Market
SITUATION #3	Favorable	Favorable	UNFAVORABLE	(c) Modify Existing Product and/or Marketing Mix for Present Market
SITUATION #4	Favorable	Favorable	Favorable	(d) No Change Required in Existing Product Design; However Improve Marketing Mix

Figure 7.5

original equipment manufacturers of automobiles, excluding the after-market for auto accessories. Let us further define the specific product types as interior and exterior flat rearview mirrors.

Moving to step 3, the trend analysis would be concerned with the performance of the firm's products of that type in the two submarkets mentioned.

Application of the Procedure

Let us now examine how the three-step procedure would be applied to the example outlined above.

Step 1. The firm would first examine the trend in *automotive rear-vision systems* in worldwide markets. Such systems might include both flat and curvilinear mirrors, combinations of mirrors, and other devices such as periscopes.

The general trend in this broadly conceived market would then be compared to the corporate product-market screening criteria. A judgment would then be made whether, all factors considered, the overall outlook is favorable in comparison with screening criteria.

If the conclusion from step 1 is that the trend comparison is unfavorable, the analysis procedure is terminated at that point. The result is classified as situation #1, Figure 7.5, and the appropriate product change would be to replace the existing product with a new product in the new market—or to diversify from that field.

In this case, there is no need to examine the submarkets (step 2) because the evaluation of submarkets and of the firm's performance in submarkets is of secondary importance, and may even be very misleading. For example, it is not uncommon for a firm, in a declining general-product field, to be misled by its short-run satisfactory performance in a submarket. Firms in this situation can be caught without suitable new product opportunities when their submarket suddenly dries up or becomes unprofitable because of intense competition due to overcapacity in the field. This situation has been observed many times by the authors, and it is especially prevalent among firms supplying the automotive and aircraft industries. It happened in the tool and die industry in the 1960's when their major customer segments shifted from buying to making a larger portion of their tools and dies.

78

Step 2. Let us assume that the result of the first-stage evaluation is favorable.

In this case the firm would move to evaluate the product trends in the major submarkets—in the example, the market among U.S. and European automotive manufacturers for interior and exterior rearview mirrors. If the analysis of the trends for these products in these markets were judged to be *unfavorable* in relation to corporate product screening criteria, the procedure would again stop. The appropriate degree of change shown in Figure 7.5 (for situation #2) would be to add a new product (line) to the present overall (auto rear-vision) market. Because the evaluation of the overall market (in step 1) has already been favorable, there is no need to diversify completely from the market, but it may be desirable to improve the product offering to the basic industry market, depending on the outcome of the step 3 analysis.

If more than one specific product or submarket is to be evaluated, such as exterior versus interior rearview mirrors for U.S. and European standard size cars versus subcompacts, the same procedure would be followed in evaluating each. Again, once an *unfavorable* result has occurred, the process stops and the degree of change for that product and submarket is indicated in the right-hand column.

Step 3. Let us now proceed to the third step by assuming that the results from the step 2 evaluations of the first submarket (interior rearview mirrors for all sizes of U.S. and European autos) were considered favorable.

In this case the analysis would proceed to evaluate the expected performance of the firm's present product offering in these interior rearview mirror markets. Here, the prime considerations are trends in market share and profit in comparison with competition (and with corporate objectives). The expected future economic potential for continuing in this market is again judged to be favorable or unfavorable.

If the result from step 3 is *unfavorable,* the evaluation process stops and the appropriate degree of product change is to modify the existing product for the same market (situation #3).

Because the trend in the interior rearview mirror submarket has already been judged to be favorable (step 2), there is no need to add a completely new product (other than rearview mirrors). The need is only to improve the existing ones, perhaps for selected segments, like subcompacts. This might be done by redesign, by cost reduction, etc., given the specific nature of the competitive situation. Further analysis to determine exactly what to do requires the procedures discussed in Chapters 10, 11, and 12.

Returning again to the example, let us assume that the result of the third-step analysis is *favorable*. In this instance we have situation #4 in Figure 7.5. For this completely favorable situation, *no* change is needed in the product. However, other changes might be desirable to serve customers more effectively with an already satisfactory product. More effective marketing, perhaps to additional segments, or better production scheduling are often the appropriate types of modification.

A Guide, Not a Panacea

There is a danger of expecting too much from any general model such as this. It must be used for the purpose intended—to give general guidance about the degree of change appropriate for the competitive situation faced. In baseball terms, the model can be described as being suitable for getting the team into the right ball park, but not for indicating precisely how to play the game.

Several limitations of the model should be recognized. First, the use of the model is dependent on the definitions chosen for the industry market and submarkets. It is not uncommon for a company to define its business focus so narrowly that the first step in the evaluation yields an unfavorable result—indicating diversification. When this happens it is often apparent that the basic definition should be broadened and the original definition should be reconsidered as a submarket of a more favorable larger product field. In this way the model can be helpful in clarifying a firm's concept of its basic business focus.

A second limitation of the model is that it considers each product or product line independently and does not take into account the interdependence of products. In some cases, products are retained to provide a total offering to the market and are not expected to produce sales and profits commensurate with corporate objectives. If it is determined that specific products need not be profitable, because of overriding market strategy, then the model is saying that some other products must make up for profit and/or return on investment which the submarginal products are not providing.

A third limitation illustrated by the preceding discussion is that the terms "product" and "product line" are not rigorously defined. This has been done intentionally because the definitions must be molded to fit the situation within different firms. In an analysis of some 100 firms in the machine tool and electronics industry, we found that most single-division firms could categorize their products into about three product lines or product-markets. The most beneficial results are achieved from the model by initially grouping the products into as few product-markets as possible, evaluating these product-markets, and then repeating the process on major individual segments within the initial product-market grouping if greater precision is needed. By redefining submarkets as sub-sub product-markets, the evaluation process may be extended to smaller and smaller individual product-market groupings, if need be.

Finally, a good deal of information is needed for the evaluations at each step in the model. Fortunately, this information is of the type that most well-managed firms have, or should have, available. Even if good information is not available, however, the model can still be used as a rough guide and can help by indicating the type of information necessary to properly evaluate new product needs.

Procedures for Evaluating New Products Are Also Useful for Existing Products

At this point in the presentation of our total procedures, we have not discussed the methods for evaluating *new* products, aside from focusing on screening criteria. It turns out, however, that both our screening criteria presented in Chapter 6 and the methods for conducting requirements research on new products (presented in Chapters 10, 11, and 12) are useful for evaluating existing products.

Existing products should be "screened" to see if they are consistent with the criteria for new products, especially regarding the matching of resources to opportunities. We have seen long-standing problems with existing products come to light by doing so. For example, a firm making specialized coatings for a segment of the scientific instrument industry suddenly realized in "screening" an existing product this way, that the reason the product line had been only marginally profitable was simply that the small market size did not provide a good match with its higher volume production equipment.

A detailed evaluation also can be made of existing products using the requirements research procedures for new products described in Chapters 10, 11, and 12. To do so, the existing product features and other elements of the market mix (the presumed target market, desired price, methods of promotion and distribution) are treated as *hypotheses* concerning how it *should* be done. The research determines whether or not the hypothesis is supported by the actual product-market requirements. Any discrepancies are used to adjust the marketing strategy for the existing product. After reading the later chapters where these techniques are described, the reader should return to this chapter and reread it to fully undersatnd the potential which the techniques offer for evaluating existing products.

Summary

Before launching new product developments, a firm should determine the extent to which objectives can be met through changes which do not involve new products. As part of its strategic planning effort each year, a quantitative and qualitative evaluation should be made of existing product market opportunities, with projections for an appropriate number of years ahead. A number of techniques are available for such evaluation developed by ourselves and others.

The output of the quantitative analysis should be a forecast of anticipated sales and profits for future years based on existing products, which, when compared to the firm's objectives, will indicate the shortfall to be made up from new products.

After the quantitative analysis has indicated the sales needed from new products, a qualitative analysis is needed to indicate the type of change needed in existing and new products to meet the desired objectives. Our techniques deal specifically with this type of evaluation. A three-step procedure was presented for determining the general type of change needed, product-market by product-market. Details on other related product evaluation methods are included in the chapters which follow.

Footnotes to Chapter 7

[1]The classic (reprint) in the field is Donald R. G. Cawan, *Sales Analysis From the Management Viewpoint* (Ann Arbor: Wolverine Publications, 1967).

[2]See also Harper W. Boyd, Jr., Ralph Westfall, and Stanley F. Stasch, *Marketing Research* (Homewood, Ill.: Richard D. Irwin, Inc., 1977), pp. 646–72.

[3]See "The Product Life Cycle: A Key to Strategic Market Planning," by John E. Smallwood, *MSU Business Topics*, Winter 1973 (E. Lansing: Michigan State University Graduate School of Business), pp. 29–35.

[4]James R. Bright, "Evaluating Signals of Technological Change," *Harvard Business Review* (Jan.–Feb., 1970), pp. 62–70.

[5]"An Advisory Council to Back Up the Board," *Business Week*, November 12, 1979, p. 131, ff.

[6]Arthur P. Lien, Paul Anton, and Joseph W. Duncan, *Technological Forecasting: Tools, Techniques, Applications*, Bulletin No. 115 (New York: American Management Association, 1968).

[7]Joseph P. Martino, "Tools for Looking Ahead," *IEEE Spectrum* (October, 1972), pp. 32–40.

[8]Laurence D. McGlouchlin, "Long Range Technical Planning," *Harvard Business Review* (July–August, 1968), pp. 54–64.

[9]James Brian Quinn, "Technological Forecasting," *Harvard Business Review* (March–April, 1967), pp. 89–106.

[10]See General Electric's "'Stoplight Strategy' for Planning," *Business Week*, April 27, 1974, p. 49.

[11]Roger A. Kerin and Robert A. Peterson, "Analytical Techniques for Strategic Marketing Management: PIMS and Boston Consulting Group Perspectives," *Perspectives on Strategic Marketing Management* (Boston: Allyn and Bacon, Inc., 1980), pp. 11–18.

[12]George S. Day, "Diagnosing the Product Portfolio," *Journal of Marketing*, Vol. 41, No. 2, April 1977, pp. 29–38.

[13]James M. Hulbert and Norman E. Toy, "A Strategic Framework for Marketing Control," *Journal of Marketing*, Vol. 41, No. 2, April 1977, pp. 12–21.

[14]Yoram Wind and Henry J. Claycamp, "Planning Product Line Strategy: A Matrix Approach," *Journal of Marketing*, Vol. 40, January 1976, pp. 2–9.

[15]One author has also recognized the limitations of the portfolio approach. See Derek F. Abell, "Strategic Windows," *Journal of Marketing*, Vol. 42, No. 3, July 1978, pp. 21–26.

[16]The initial model developed included possible combinations of three changes in product, three changes in process, two changes in market, and two changes in price. See: "Research on Product Development Capabilities of Michigan Firms," by Frank R. Bacon, Jr., and Frederick T. Sparrow, *Papers of the Michigan Academy of Science, Arts and Letters*, XLVII Part II, Social Science, 1963, pp. 341–356.

UNDERSTAND
DIVISIONAL GOALS
WHAT CAN GET US WHAT?

SECTION THREE

NEW PRODUCT DEVELOPMENT
PROCEDURES

Chapter 8

Overview of New Product Procedures

When examination of the strategic considerations indicates the need for new products, other procedures are required to identify and evaluate potential new product opportunities. The chapters in the present section are devoted to such procedures.

Relationships among the chapters and procedures are shown in Figure 8.1.

The first step is to obtain new product ideas or opportunities (Chapter 9), then screen the ideas using the criteria already developed (Chapter 6). Potential new opportunities which pass the screen must be given priorities for subsequent evaluation, usually by an executive committee or new products committee as discussed later in Chapter 13. Evaluation is accomplished in the multistage process we call "requirements research," discussed in Chapters 10, 11, and 12.

The output from requirements research may be to proceed with technical and (subsequently) market development, or to go into a "hold" until a major problem is resolved or an anticipated event takes place. For example, the project may be put on hold because the size of computer memory available at current costs may not meet requirements. The decision may be to await further developments in memory technology before proceeding. On the market side, a hold may be justified because the size of the market may be too small to justify entry at this time, but is expected to grow in relation to the growth of a related product. For example, the size of the market for low-cost keyboards is related to the growth of the home computer market. When necessary events have occurred, the project is reviewed and reactivated.

When the output of the requirements research stages is positive, the new product concept proceeds through technical development, engineering, and manufacture, all the while being guided by the requirements research and being coordinated in various ways by the new products committee or related personnel.

87

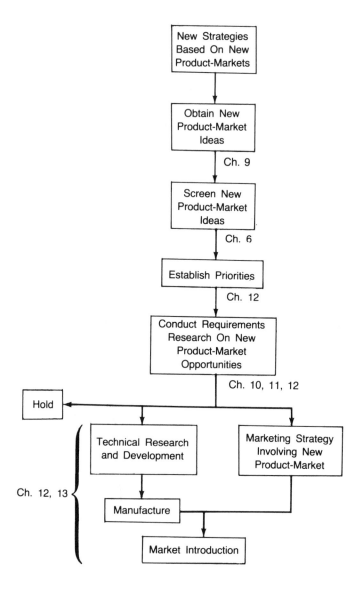

Figure 8.1 Implementation Through New Product Innovation.

The requirements research is also a key ingredient in formulating the marketing strategy and the market introduction plan. We suggest that personnel responsible for new products be involved in a coordination role in these marketing-related activities as well, as

88

explained in Chapters 13 and 14, which address new product introduction, organization, and staffing issues.

Relationships among the activities will become more meaningful as we discuss the procedures used at each stage in the overall process, to which we now turn.

Chapter 9

Obtaining New Product Ideas

Before starting to look for ideas, we should first decide what it is we are looking for. What makes a new product idea a "good" one? Reduced to its most elemental form, a "good" new product idea is simply the solution to a customer's problem, done in such a way that both the customer and the supplying firm reach their own individual objectives (sales, profit). Thus, a user's problem and a supplier's market opportunity may be considered opposite sides of the same coin.

Given this basic definition of a good new product, one can thus see why the process of generating new product ideas might be enhanced by distributing the new product's screening criteria to key personnel within the firm as discussed earlier in Chapter 6. The criteria provide a broad focus on the types of problems and resources available for problem solving, which if properly matched, will likely result in meeting the firm's own objectives. As we now turn to the traditional sources of new product ideas, it will be no surprise to learn that the best sources have been those who are either familiar with customer needs and problems or knowledgeable about new technical solutions to existing or new problems.

Internal Sources of New Product Ideas

The principal internal sources of new product ideas are shown in Figure 9.1. The two major sources are from personnel in marketing and in research, development, and engineering. Personnel in manufacturing constitutes a third, and logically less significant, source of new product ideas. Within marketing, personnel in frequent contact with customers and users are in a good position to spot problems which can be converted into new product opportunities. This is especially true of salesmen and applica-

INTERNAL SOURCES OF NEW PRODUCT IDEAS

From:

Marketing
- Product Managers
- Salesmen
- Applications Engineers
- Installers
- Servicemen, Warranty Claims, Failure Records

Research, Development, and Engineering
- Product Designers
- Materials Engineers
- Process Engineers

Production
- Methods Engineers
- Quality Control and Testing
- Packaging

Other

Figure 9.1

tions engineers. However, others in frequent contact with customers such as installers and servicemen are in an excellent position to see where the existing product does not meet the entire need of the customer, or where it might be modified or the product line extended to better meet the total need. Ideas for needed improvements in existing products are also frequently generated by analysis of warranty claims and failure records.

It is logical that personnel in research, development, and engineering constitute a second major source of new product ideas. Product designers, materials engineers, and process engineers are daily concerned with new technical solutions and materials for the design and processing of existing and new products. Although the new product development process should ideally start with the identification of a customer need followed by the development of the appropriate technical solution, many new product opportunities have started from a technological breakthrough in the research laboratory followed by discovery of appropriate market applications.

Personnel in production, such as methods engineers and personnel engaged in quality control, testing, and packaging are often overlooked as sources of new product ideas. However, these personnel are in an excellent position to suggest ways to improve existing products or to make a logical extension of the present product line. In summary, ideas for new products can come internally from *anyone familiar with customer needs and problems* or with potential technical solutions which can be converted into new products or improvements in existing ones.

External Sources of New Products

Sources of new product ideas external to the firm fall into two major groupings similar to those discussed above for internal sources. These groupings, shown in Figure 9.2, include persons aware of customer needs and problems and those aware of new technical solutions to existing or new problems.

Customers and users themselves are a prime source of information concerning new problems and needs. Other marketing intermediaries such as distributors, agents, and dealers are also in

---

EXTERNAL SOURCES OF NEW PRODUCT IDEAS

Reflecting Awareness of Customer Need:
- Customers
- Distributor and Dealers
- User Panels
- Focus Groups
- Competitors' Products
- Consultants

Reflecting Awareness of New Technical Solutions:
- Patent Attorneys, Files
- Licensors
- Independent Inventors
- Materials Suppliers
- Research Labs, Universities
- Technical Consultants

Figure 9.2

an excellent position to learn of customer problems which need addressing. Consultants who are dealing with customers or marketing channel members are likewise in a position to learn of customer problems which need to be addressed, and to suggest possible solutions.

And ideas for new products can come from the examination of competitors' product lines. There are several traps to avoid, however, such as developing "me-too" products with insufficient differential competitive advantage, or following a competitor in developing a new product for which there is insufficient market demand. Both of these problems can be avoided by conducting adequate market requirements research such as described in later chapters.

Ideas for new products can come from a wide range of technical sources. These include patent attorneys, independent investors, materials suppliers, research laboratories, universities, and technical consultants. Regular use of external technical sources is one means of maintaining fresh creative technical solutions and avoiding the well-known "Not Invented Here" (NIH) syndrome. This is one of the characteristics that distinguished successful from unsuccessful new product developments in the "Project SAPPHO" study mentioned in Chapter 1.[1]

Stimulating Sources of New Product Ideas

Experience has shown that both internal and external sources of ideas can be stimulated. During the past ten years a good deal of attention has been focused on the ideation process and the development of techniques for stimulating creativity.[2] The amount of stimulation required depends on the amount of new product ideas needed. We have observed in instances where a structured procedure for new product development has not been in operation that the establishment of new product evaluation procedures and the announcement that new ideas are solicited will start an immediate flow of ideas. Many people such as application engineers, servicemen, materials engineers, and quality control supervisors have simply never been urged to submit ideas. Ideas are stimulated simply by giving these people information about the type of solution desired, such as was outlined in the screening criteria, and assuring them that all ideas will be treated fairly and objectively.

In a similar vein, ideas from customers, distributors, and dealers can be stimulated by encouraging sales personnel, applications engineers, and service men to ask customers and distributors about their problems and needs in the normal course of their contact with these people.

In instances where a significant lack of ideas exists, the establishment of ideation procedures such as periodic brainstorming sessions can be an effective stimulant.[3] One such procedure we have used successfully is to have a total of six to ten people assembled for one to two hours in a session which includes the director of new product development. For maximum stimulation it is important that personnel be present from different functional areas of the business such as sales, application engineering, product design, process engineering, etc. This session simply focuses on customer problems and needs which might be served by the company with existing or new technology. Suggestions should be received in a noncritical, nonevaluative mode with discussions limited to clarification of the concept. No judgmental discussion should take place at such sessions.

Following the sessions, the director of new product development evaluates the ideas, using the new product screen and informs the person who originated the idea whether the idea passed the screen or not, and if not, what aspects of the screen the product did not meet. After several iterations of meetings of this kind, personnel in attendance become attuned to the type of new product idea which the firm can use.

If the firm or division has established a technical board (see Appendix), this group also can be used to evaluate current product and process technology and suggest alternative technical solutions for improved or new products. The use of value analysis is an effective way to stimulate ideas concerning reduction in cost through product and process changes, especially when the product is in the mature stage of its product life cycle.

If sufficient ideas are not stimulated through these activities, efforts should be made to broaden the outside contacts made by persons in all functional areas—marketing, engineering, and production, possibly with the assistance of consulting firms. Typical increased activities include attending more association meetings and trade shows, participating in technical symposia, technical expositions, and conferences. The number of these activities must be increased until the number of new product ideas is sufficient to provide the sales and profits needed to meet the firm's objectives. A conscientious program of this nature can produce dramatic results.

Summary

In this chapter we have shown that a good new product idea is one which results in the solution of a customer's problem at a profit to the supplying firm. Ideas for new products come mainly from those in contact with customer needs such as salesmen and application engineers, but also from those aware of new technical solutions to problems such as engineers and research personnel. External to the firm, customers and distributors and dealers who serve the firm can be major sources of new product ideas as can be independent inventors, university staff, and technical consultants who may provide new technical information to the firm. There are a number of techniques which can be successfully used to stimulate the flow of new ideas. They all involve increased awareness of customer needs and problems and/or awareness of new technical solutions. In most instances, we have found that dissemination and explanation of screening criteria alone provide the stimulus for the generation of an adequate number of worthwhile product ideas.

Footnotes to Chapter 9

[1]C. Freeman, et al., "Success and Failure in Industrial Innovation" [Project SAPPHO]. Centre for the Study of Industrial Innovation, The University of Sussex, England, 1972.

[2]See, for example: E. Patrick McGuire, *Generating New Product Ideas* (The Conference Board, Inc., 1977); W. J. J. Gordon, *Synectics* (New York: Harper and Row, 1976); S. J. Parnes, R. B. Noller, and A. M. Biondi, *Guide to Creative Actions* (Buffalo: Creative Education Foundation, 1977); and "Survey of Creativity Methods," *Dun's Review*, January 1980.

[3]*Ibid.*, especially Parnes, *et al.*

Chapter 10

Analyzing Requirements for New Products:
The General Procedure

After new product ideas have been obtained as discussed in the previous chapter, they must be evaluated, first with the screening criteria (Chapter 6), and second with detailed research procedures (to determine the total requirements for a successful innovation). Ideas which initially do not pass the screen, of course, receive no further evaluation. And if several new product concepts pass the screen, each must be assigned priorities for the further, more detailed investigation. Priorities are usually established by top management, as we mentioned in Chapter 6.

The present chapter will describe the *general* procedures used in the detailed requirements research which follows the successful completion of the screening step. In the next two chapters we present the *specific* techniques, the choice of which depends largely on the economic and emotive bases of need for the new product. Since the two most prevalent situations involve (1) either products with primarily economic motives, or (2) products where emotive motives predominate, we present techniques used in each case. Situations involving a balance between the two types of motives are also addressed.

The Model of Requirements for
Successful Innovation

Analysis of new product requirements employs the model of "Requirements for Successful Innovation," shown in Figures 10.1, 10.2, 10.5, 10.7, and 10.8. The total requirement for successful innovation is viewed in Figure 10.1 as the simultaneous solution of multiple requirements grouped in five principal domains: (1) the marketing requirements domain, (2) the physical requirements domain, (3) the resources requirements domain, (4) the economic

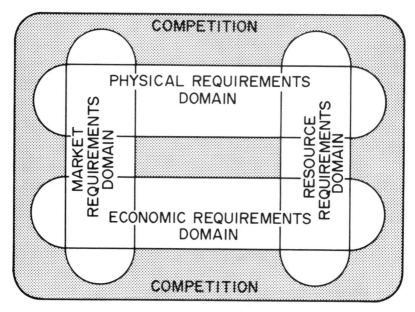

Figure 10.1   Total Requirements for Successful Innovation.

requirements domain, and (5) the competitive requirements domain.

The Market Requirements Domain

Analysis of customer need is the key task involved in determining requirements in the market requirements domain shown in Figure 10.2. Three principal areas need to be investigated. The first is the physical requirement of the product or service to meet the total customer need (the intersection of the market and physical requirements domains). If a product such as an electronic digital scale for counting parts by weight is being evaluated it would be necessary to identify the size of parts, weights, shapes, and quantities which will need to be counted. The digital parts-counting scale shown in Figure 10.3 was designed using these procedures.

The second aspect requiring analysis is the source of value associated with the need, especially the values attributable to different need-satisfying elements (the intersection of the market and economic requirements domains in Figure 10.2). For the

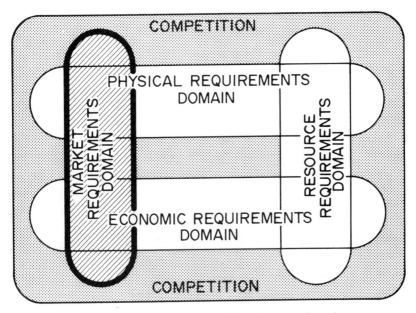

Figure 10.2 The Market Requirements Domain.

Figure 10.3 Toledo Scale's Digital Parts-Counting Scale.

99

digital parts counting scale, it would be necessary to determine the source and amount of value associated with the direct labor cost savings possible with a faster process, or the value from increased production due to better parts control, or from not having to close a plant or retail store as long as was previously necessary to take a complete inventory. There may be additional value from having features such as automatic tare adjustment, printout, tie-in to a central computer, or availability of a maintenance contract. These are separate need-satisfying elements whose requirements and value would have to be assessed before designing the equipment.

The third aspect needing investigation is the possible sources of competitive advantage which may be derived from serving customer needs better than competitors are doing (the intersection of the entire market domain with the domain of competition in Figure 10.2). That advantage often is found in designing a product to better meet all aspects of the total need, thus resulting in greater value to the customer for the same or lower price. In the case of the digital scale, this might be the ability to count parts at lower cost than with existing methods.

The development engineer must understand how much better (faster, smaller, etc.) the product must be in comparison to competition and what value is attached to various attributes in order to optimize the product design.

Outputs from these aspects of the total investigation are a principal input in determining the design parameters for the new product. Remember that a "product" is viewed as "the summation of all need-satisfying elements," and may include a physical device or a service as we have mentioned above. For example, the product could be a service, such as janitorial services in large commercial buildings or in private homes. In this case the physical requirements for the service must be determined: what is to be cleaned, how often, with what materials, etc., together with the associated value for each element in order to design the product offering.

When designing a completely new product, such as the first electronic counter-scale used in supermarkets and at candy counters, as shown in Figure 10.4, or the first automatic mail delivery vehicle for large office buildings, the customer may have almost no idea what the new product or special features of the product will be worth. Yet the development engineer needs reasonably accurate selling price information as a design require-

Figure 10.4   Toledo Scale's Electronic Counter-Scale.

ment. One of the key features of the approach we have developed is the technique which permits assessing the value of possible new product attributes in circumstances such as these. The technique is explained later in the present chapter and illustrated further in Chapters 11 and 12.

The Physical Requirements Domain

Requirements in the physical domain shown in Figure 10.5 are defined mainly by the intersection of the domain with three others: the market, resource, and competitive requirements domains. In starting the analysis of requirements for a new product, it is advantageous to begin with the intersection of the market and

101

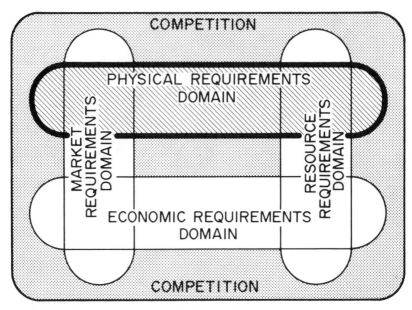

Figure 10.5   The Physical Requirements Domain.

physical requirements domains. The output of this aspect is the specification of the physical requirements to meet the user need, as discussed above.

This information facilitates the analysis of the intersection of the physical and resource requirements domains, as well. The fundamental question addressed here is, what are the technical options which might be used to meet the physical requirements, which are within the resources of the firm, and which will offer some protection from competitive reaction (possibly a patent or proprietary production process)? If possible the firm would like to find a unique technical solution to the physical requirement. Quite often the competitive distinction between firms serving the same markets will lie in different technologies which are not within the different capabilities of all firms. Therefore, in evaluating the technical requirements it is of utmost importance to recognize which technologies to be used are within the resources of the firm and (let us hope) not within those of competitors.

For example, in making the transition from mechanical to electronic scales, the Toledo Scale Division of Reliance Electric

102

Company enjoyed a strong competitive advantage for several years, because it was able to pioneer in the combination of strain-gauge and microprocessor technologies. Similarly, AMF was able to obtain the dominant position in the field of automatic scoring in bowling with its "MagicScore"[R] system due to its capability to apply sonar technology to acoustical sensing of bowling pins (see Figure 10.6). The technology, which came from years of involvement with national defense contracts, resulted in a strong patent position.

As can be imagined, this aspect of the analysis of requirements for a given product innovation can involve extensive technical investigation, possibly over a period of many months.

The Resource Requirements Domain

In parallel with the technical design requirements, the firm needs to understand the other resource requirements for success with the innovation. This domain is illustrated in Figure 10.7. The major resource requirements are defined by the intersection of this domain with the physical, economic, and competitive requirements domains. The intersection of the physical and resource re-

Figure 10.6   AMF's MagicScore[H] System in Operation.

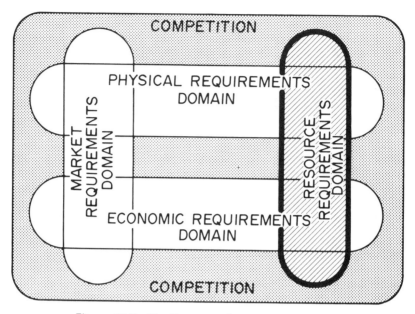

Figure 10.7 The Resource Requirements Domain.

quirements domains defines the technical design requirements as discussed above.

The intersection of the resource and economic domains is where the issues of adequate production technology, capacity, economies of scale, management, and financial strength are examined. It is also where the marketing requirements must be examined to ascertain that they are within the firm's capability. For example, the new product may require establishing a national service organization, or may require large amounts of multimedia national advertising, neither of which is within the firm's resource capability.

The output from this phase of the requirements research provides a positive check on whether there is or can be a good match of the firm's resources, both qualitative and quantitative, to the opportunity under study. It also provides information about how well the firm's strengths or weaknesses compare with those of potential competitors. For example, in considering the development of the "MagicScore"[R] system, AMF was already dominant in the bowling field, had the necessary broad technical base to evaluate the many technical approaches possible, and had a competent service organization already in place. Thus, the decision to introduce a high-technology product to this field represented—in total—a good matching of resources to opportunity.

The Economic Requirements Domain

Ultimate success is measured by the bottom line. The basic economic requirements are defined by the intersection of this domain with the resource, market and competitive requirements domains as shown in Figure 10.8. Simply stated, if the innovation is to be a commercial success, the product must be produced and marketed at a cost less than its value in the eyes of the customer. There must be adequate profit. In comparison to competitive offerings, the product must produce a superior value for the functions served. This may or may not be done with a lower selling price. The analysis of competitive product features and prices is an important aspect of this phase of the requirements research. In achieving its growth to number one position in pro-shop sales of golf clubs, as mentioned previously, Ben Hogan clubs with the "Legend" shaft were priced at a premium.

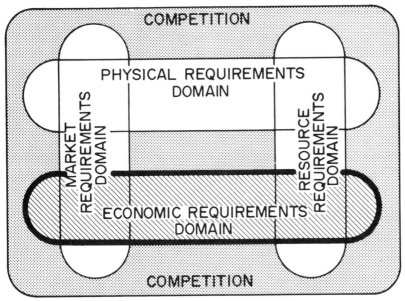

Figure 10.8   The Economic Requirements Domain.

The Competitive Requirements Domain

The competitive domain intersects and surrounds all other domains as shown in the previous figures. It is depicted in this manner, because a competitive advantage may occur in any domain. The product may have superior physical attributes because it better meets the needs. It may use better technology. It may be produced to yield higher quality, or produced at a lower price. It may provide greater value in use to the customer, or the marketing and distribution, service capability, etc., may provide distinct competitive advantages.

Many small firms do not recognize the protection afforded to their larger competitors by the dominant market position held by many large firms. This is especially true with introduction of dramatically new products. Consider, for example, how difficult it would have been for a small unknown firm to introduce the first solid dietary snack bar, Figurines[R], introduced successfully by Pillsbury (discussed in detail in Chapter 12).

Since a competitive advantage can be found in any of the domains, all must be examined. No product development should proceed unless the basis for competitive advantage can be identified *prior to technical development,* and has been judged to be adequate.

The degree of competitive advantage required depends largely on the relative strengths of the firm and its competitors. A small firm competing with much larger ones may insist on strong proprietary advantage in the form of a patent or secret production process. A large firm may be able to rely solely on its prior market strength, its image in the market, or greater economy of scale in production facilities, even with very little physical product differentiation. Although the degree of competitive advantage required will differ from situation to situation, the basis should be identified and assessed for adequacy prior to technical and market development.

In summary, this conceptual model provides a *framework* for guiding the analysis and investigating work needed to determine whether a new product opportunity can be converted into a successful new product innovation.

In addition to its use in evaluating new opportunities, the model can be used to audit existing business (as mentioned in

Chapter 7), and to analyze why unsuccessful new product ventures have not achieved the success predicted, as discussed later in the present chapter. The model also has great value in providing continued guidance concerning whether changes are required (in physical attributes, in technology, in marketing, pricing, etc.) throughout the new product development process or to redirect an existing new product effort toward success. Other specific techniques are, of course, needed to make the conceptual model operational. They will be discussed next.

Procedures for Applying the Conceptual Model

In utilizing the model of requirements for successful innovation shown in Figures 10.1, 10.2, 10.5, 10.7, and 10.8, it is convenient to focus on the *intersections* of the five domains as illustrated in Figure 10.9. Each intersection is systematically investigated to evaluate a new product opportunity.

Recall that there are six areas which must be studied. These include the four corners, which actually represent five areas of analysis since the lower right-hand corner includes both production and distribution (marketing) methods which are conveniently separated for analysis. The sixth segment is competition, which intersects with all of the other five areas.

Questions to be Answered About Each Segment of the Model

We have determined that four questions provide adequate direction for the research activities into the six areas of the model. These questions include the following:

1. How is the function performed now (for which the new product or service is expected to provide improvement)?
2. What does the present method cost?
3. What is wrong with the present method and what improvements are needed in present methods?
4. What value would the improvements have (to the intended user)?

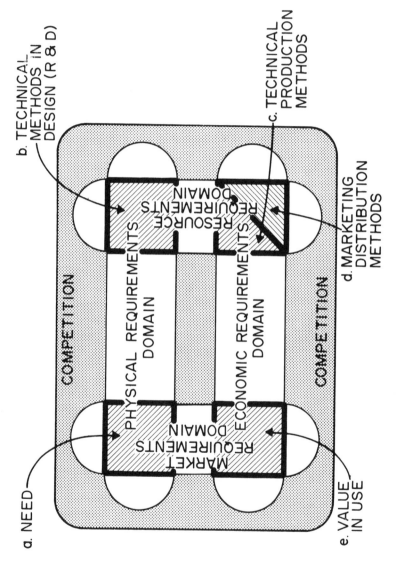

Figure 10.9   Segments of Requirements for which Separate Analysis is Possible.

108

When the four framework questions are applied to the segments, the result is a matrix of information requirements shown in schematic form in Figure 10.10. The full matrix thus includes all the information required to make the complete model operational. The four questions are shown as columns in the figure, and four segments of the conceptual model are shown as rows. Questions 1 and 3 provide the basic focus for the investigation in each of the six segments, which cover the physical, market, and resource requirements (technical design, production, and marketing). The economic requirements (economic value and cost considerations) are included in the application of questions 2 and 4 to the other four segments. The competitive environment is treated

INFORMATION REQUIREMENTS

	How is Basic Function Performed Now?	What Do Present Methods Cost?	What's Wrong With Present Method?	What Value Improvements Have
A. Physical Need				
B. Technical Product Design (R&D)				
C. Technical Production Process Methods				
D. Marketing & Distribution Methods				
E. Economic Cost & Value Consideration				

Figure 10.10

as a specific aspect in the analysis of each segment (row) of the matrix.

The information required to complete the full matrix is too complex to illustrate in one chart. For this reason we present the detailed information requirements in Figures 10.11 through 10.14. Each table represents typical information needed in one row of the schematic matrix shown in Figure 10.10.

Figure 10.11 presents the information needed about physical requirements (segment A); Figure 10.12, information about technical requirements (segment B); Figure 10.13, information about production and process requirements (segment C); and Figure 10.14 contains information needed about marketing and distribution requirements (segment D). Economic costs and value considerations (segment E) are considered within each of the segments A through D. The four framework questions provide an outline for the detailed information which must be obtained about each of the segments of requirements. The detailed questions shown in the series of figures are typical for most products, but some variation can be expected, depending on the particular product under study.

Some redundancy is both necessary and desirable to cover each segment from an independent viewpoint. For example, the technical aspects of product design overlap the technical aspects of production methods. But both points of view must be considered—the costs associated with R&D and design must be balanced against the costs of production using various materials (e.g., plastic vs. metal). Both must, of course, be considered in light of the physical market requirements, including warranty or service required to be competitive.

The analysis of competition is included within the matrix of information required. This information may be, and often is, recombined for greater emphasis into a separate report on the competitive situation anticipated.

The Need for a Detailed Approach

Rather than obtain all the information outlined in Figures 10.11–10.14, one might wonder why it is not possible simply to ask potential customers if they would like the new product under consideration and what they would be willing to pay for it. In a few

TYPICAL INFORMATION REQUIRED
CONCERNING PHYSICAL NEED
[Row (A) in Schematic Matrix, Figure 10.10]

1. How is it (physically) done now? How are basic functions (physically) performed? What products are now used?
   a. Describe methods used now; use flow diagrams.
   b. What equipment is used?
   c. What labor skills are used?
   d. What materials and suppliers are used?
2. What does it cost now to perform the basic function?
   a. Cost in each step of flow diagrams.
   b. Cost of equipment.
   c. Cost of labor; include fringe and overhead.
   d. Cost of materials and supplies.
   e. Other costs.
   f. Determine what measure of unit cost would be suitable, comparing different products in cost per part, per pound, per hour, etc.
   g. Are products standard or must they be built to order?
3. What is wrong with present product or method; what are major and minor problems and why are these problems?
   a. What improvements are needed in the way the function is physically done now and why; could a better method be used?
   b. Does method need to be faster, more reliable, more durable, produce higher quality, more accurate parts, etc.?
   c. Could product or method be expanded to other uses if certain changes or improvements could be made?
4. What value would improvements have (in the way the function is physically done now)?
   a. For each problem or possible improvement:
      (1) Identify amount of potential cost savings over existing method and explain why.
      (2) Identify any additional values (which may be intangible)—more efficient process, management time savings, ease of installation, etc. Identify reason for additional value and possible means for quantifying it.

Figure 10.11

111

1. How is it done now (technical design and development)?
   a. What are principal technical components or ingredients used in product now (solid-state, MSI, LSI)?
   b. What technology is used in each major component or ingredient (in helical worm gears, laser metrology)?
   c. What skills or equipment are needed for design and development?
      (1) Artistic drafting?
      (2) Computer optimization of design?
      (3) Special testing facility?
   d. What specialists are now used—chemists, physicists?
      (1) Levels of education?
2. What does it cost now (to design and develop)?
   a. Cost of labor skills required?
   b. Cost of lab equipment?
   c. Cost of testing facility?
   d. Cost of licenses, if any?
3. What is wrong with the technical design and/or procedures used in the design process?
   a. What technical improvements are needed (or possible) in *product*?
   b. Small package?
   c. Is a different technology being used for the same function (strain gauges instead of mechanical scale) (LSI instead of MSI)?
   d. Thicker coating for greater durability, etc.?
4. What is the value of technical improvements?
   a. Better performance for same or lower cost (what is value of better performance; how to measure—lighter weight = fuel savings)?
   b. Are new uses possible with new technology (value = sales in new market)?

Figure 10.12

cases this is possible, such as when a minor modification has been made in an existing product. In this situation the customer has a sufficient understanding of the product and its use to provide useful information.

But what if the product simply does not exist or represents a major departure from existing methods, as is often the case with a

---

TYPICAL INFORMATION REQUIRED CONCERNING
PRODUCTION/PROCESS METHODS
[Row (C) in Schematic Matrix, Figure 10.10]

1. How is it manufactured now?
   a. Typical size (production lot).
   b. Flow diagram of production sequence from operation to operation.
   c. Size of plants used.
   d. Key equipment needed in production.
   e. Labor skills used and amount of each.
   f. Where plants are located.
   g. Total volume of production in recent years.
   h. Supplier sources used.
   i. Methods used in purchasing.
2. What does product cost to manufacture now?
   a. From price of product to highest volume and lowest volume users, estimate manufacturing cost.
   b. Cost ot plant used.
   c. Cost of equipment, building, electricity, supplies, labor skills, etc.
   d. What other products are also made at same plant and/or with same equipment?
   e. What is purchase cost of major components (motors, spindle drives)?
3. What is wrong with the methods of manufacture?
   a. Where do problems arise in product due to production techniques?
   b. Improved quality control needed? If so, what size, color, etc.?
   c. Is larger volume of production needed?
   d. Is faster delivery on special orders needed?
   e. Are better castings needed, better paint, etc.?
   f. Is better packaging needed?
4. What would value of improvements in production methods be and why?
   a. Where would greatest value or cost savings originate (from fewer returned items—due to *what*; cracking, poor soldering, etc.)?
   b. Are any cost savings due to better production process (less maintenance)?
   c. Is any lower cost possible from improving equipment in plant? From having a larger scale?

Figure 10.13

TYPICAL INFORMATION REQUIRED CONCERNING
MARKETING AND DISTRIBUTION METHODS
[Row (D) in Schematic Matrix, Figure 10.10]

1. How is marketing done now?
   a. What markets are served now; segmented by industries, geographic areas, demographics?
   b. What channels are used now; percentage of sales to each—direct, reps., distributors?
   c. Where is stocking done now at which level—where geographically?
   d. What promotion is used now?
   e. What is method of shipping used; who pays freight?
   f. What type of warranty is on product?
   g. How is maintenance service handled?
   h. Who pays for returned merchandise?
2. What does marketing and distribution cost now?
   a. Discount structure at each level in distribution channel; any extra discount for stocking distributor?
   b. Shipping cost?
   c. Costs due to breakage, returned goods?
   d. Cost of promotion—ads, literature?
   e. Service costs—who pays?
3. What is wrong with the marketing and distribution now?
   a. Need faster delivery on standard or special items?
   b. Frequency of out-of-stock? On what type or model of product?
   c. Greater variety needed in color, size?
   d. Better maintenance? Faster, better quality?
   e. Does manufacturer do a poor job in servicing accounts, providing information, technical assistance; does he need more promotion to distributor, user?
   f. Are production complaints handled promptly by manufacturer?
4. What value would improvements in marketing and distribution methods have?
   a. Are there lost orders because of out-of-stock or delivery? If so, how many and value of them per year?
   b. Lower cost possible due to better maintenance by manufacturer—number of service calls saved (reduced) per year?
   c. Does distributor have to promote product locally, which could be done by manufacturer with cost savings to distributor? How many dollars are involved per year; i.e., does distributor have to print literature, etc.?

Figure 10.14

new product opportunity? The customers may have little idea whether they want the device and no basis for estimating the price they would be willing to pay for it. In such cases, the investigation of the physical need segment and economic value-cost segments of Figure 10.10 will disclose potential customers who can provide direct answers only of the type covered by the first framework question: (1) "How is it done now?"

Although they may be aware of the elements of cost associated with the present method (Question 2), they are often unaware of the total present cost. And when dramatic new procedures are introduced, such as electronic counting of parts by weighing or numerical control of machine tools, there may be large indirect cost savings, of which the user has no prior knowledge. For these reasons, the total cost of the present system usually must be "pieced together" by the researcher. It is not a simple task of getting a direct answer to the question.

Potential users often have not given serious thought to the third and fourth questions: (3) "What is wrong with the present method? and (4) "What value would improvements have?" because they are unaware of possible new methods for satisfying the need. However, they can usually be stimulated to think about deficiencies in the present methods, and valuable responses almost always are obtained. Answers to the fourth question, on the other hand, are more difficult to obtain until the user understands the new equipment or system. However, the researcher again can "piece together" the additional value by identifying the sources of value, such as management time freed for other tasks, and by estimating the magnitude of each component of value.

This was the case when electronic numerical control of machine tools was first developed. Potential users could explain how they set up and operated conventional machines, the precision obtained, and the costs and production output. But they were not able to fully understand how automatic positioning and control would affect setup times and operation and what additional value it would have in comparison with conventional methods. However, the researcher could obtain the equipment costs, setup times, run time, number of pieces produced, percentage of scrap produced, etc., associated with the present procedures, and then, being familiar with possible new technologies, could estimate the savings possible with new procedures, even though the potential customer did not have sufficient knowledge to do so.

It is also important to note that the researcher does not need to know the details of the new technical approach to obtain the basic present cost information, or even to identify potential sources of additional value. At the investigation stage the researcher can operate on general hypotheses regarding the benefits likely from a proposed new approach to the basic function(s). The development of the Mailmobile[R] system by Lear Siegler, Inc., shown in Figure 10.15, for delivery of mail, documents, supplies, etc. in the office environment (mentioned at the end of Chapter 6) is an excellent case in point. In studying the basic office delivery function, the researchers had only a general concept concerning the actual equipment design, yet the elements of present cost and

Figure 10.15   The Mailmobile[R] Vehicle.

additional value were identified in the investigation to guide subsequent technical development activities.

Investigation May Start in Any Domain

Each of the segments of the basic model can be systematically researched independently of the others. However, greatest efficiency in new product development usually occurs when the analysis of the physical value requirements (market need) can be completed before a large expenditure on research and engineering has been made. As mentioned earlier, the ability to provide meaningful direction to research and engineering is one of the strongest features of our method. Actually, one cannot proceed very far toward defining the technical requirements until the physical performance and economic parameters have been defined.

Ideally the procedure should start with the analysis of physical and economic requirements, followed by analysis of technical, manufacturing, and marketing requirements, and then competition. However, the method can be initiated in any sequence, and at any stage of an already existing development project. In many instances a technical breakthrough will initiate the process. Market requirements and competition then must be properly defined before further technical development can proceed. If some segments of the matrix have already been adequately researched, they need not be duplicated, and the researcher can move on to check the requirements in other areas. In this way the probability of success of ongoing products can be enhanced by using portions of the procedure.

Evaluation of Existing Products

Additionally, if products have been introduced to the market with marginal success, it is possible to use the same method to evaluate why the new product is not achieving its anticipated success. In this mode, the existing product, price, techniques of manufacture and marketing are considered to be hypotheses about the requirements to meet the market need and achieve a competitive advantage.

The same type of investigation can be carried out without presenting or discussing the existing new product with users or customers. The requirements for successful innovation can be determined independently and then compared with the previously developed product, including price, manufacturing method, and marketing program. Discrepancies between the required and existing product, or required and existing marketing and production programs signal the type of changes needed for success. We have assisted a number of firms with studies of this type. Typically, the lack of success is related to improper identification of physical and economic requirements in the initial development effort. This often results in the development of a product which meets the needs of only a narrow segment of the total market—thus leading to less than anticipated sales.

Analysis of Competition

To obtain success with an innovation, the product or service must meet the requirements of the market place, and must utilize appropriate technical, manufacturing, and marketing methods to deliver the product at the appropriate price and costs. These are necessary, but not sufficient, conditions for economic succcess. Sufficiency requires, in addition, that adequate protection be achieved in some way to permit the innovation to enjoy success long enough to produce the necessary return on investment.

Competitive advantage may be realized in any of the five areas depicted as the corners of the basic requirements model (Figure 10.9). The advantage may lie in better meeting the physical need, in superior design technology, in materials, in lower-cost production, or in more effective marketing. One, or a combination of advantages may be found. The key to finding the advantage is to analyze all aspects of potential competitive advantage before the technical development is launched.

The competitive analysis focuses primarily on answering the first three framework questions about each of the major competitors: (1) How is it done now? (2) What does it cost now? and (3) What is wrong with the present method? This means studying the competing products, technologies, and manufacturing and marketing methods and ascertaining prices and costs to the extent possible. Although it may not be possible to visit competitors' manufacturing facilities, it is usually possible to inspect the competing product, obtain literature with performance specifications, or even purchase the product and disassemble it. Manufacturing

118

costs usually can be estimated from inspection of component parts (stampings, castings, etc.) together with estimates of sales volume.

Users of competing products usually are willing to demonstrate the product and discuss the advantages and disadvantages. However, one must be aware that users tend to defend their purchase decisions, and are no longer completely objective in their evaluations.

In a similar way, marketing and distribution costs can be estimated by learning what channels and promotional materials are being used and applying traditional mark-ups or cost ratios to estimated sales. It is especially important to assess the market position already obtained by competition within each major segment of potential markets. Again, this information has greatest value if it is available to guide initial product developments and market strategy formulation.

An Approach That Goes Beyond Current Awareness

The information presented in the figures above, and the procedures described in the following chapters are designed to *go beyond* the potential user's current awareness of his need and of the value of its fulfillment. This is accomplished by prestructuring the research to obtain answers for all four framework questions in all segments of the models.

To do so, the researcher must know what information he needs about each domain (as illustrated in Figures 10.11–10.14) and must be willing to dig it out. If the work is carefully done, it is not unreasonable to obtain adequate information for the design of a product whose need and value have not been fully recognized by the potential customers (or competitors). Yet customers can be expected to purchase a product readily when its usefulness and value is demonstrated and when it is priced according to its value.

We next turn our attention to the research procedures needed to get the information which has been outlined in the above figures.

The Role of Hypotheses

Hypotheses play an important role in any disciplined research effort. Unfortunately, the term has an "academic" connotation among practical businessmen. As we shall demonstrate in this and later chapters, however, hypotheses are of extreme practical importance in the new product investigation process. Many businessmen, once they have experienced our disciplined research approach to new products, have urged us to give greater stress to the value of hypotheses in the research process when describing the process to others.

The overall role of hypotheses in the Bacon-Butler research process is illustrated in Figure 10.16. Following the arrows down

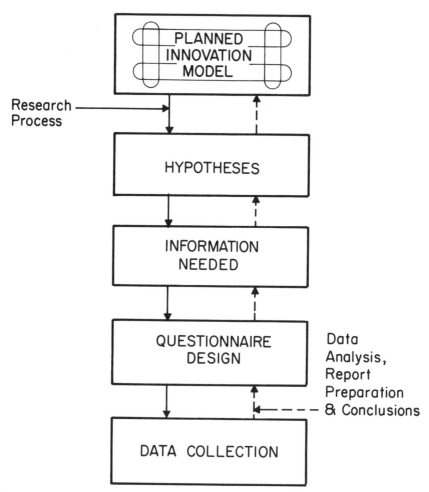

Figure 10.16   Relationship of Planned Innovation Model to Hypotheses and Data Collection.

the left side of the figure, you can see that hypotheses generated are based on the corners of the requirements model shown at the top of the figure. The hypotheses define what information needs to be collected, with specific reference to the basic requirements model. A questionnaire or other research procedure is then designed to obtain the needed information.

Now follow the arrows up the right side of the figure. After the questionnaire is used to get the information, the hypotheses provide a framework for relating the diverse pieces of data to the requirements model at the top. In many instances the hypotheses form a suitable outline for writing the associated research reports.

The reader familiar with scientific procedures will recognize that Figure 10.16 embodies the scientific method. The Bacon-Butler requirements model at the top of the figure could be replaced with any other model or theoretical framework and the figure would illustrate the scientific method of conducting research. Thus, what we have attempted to do is to construct a useful model of requirements for successful innovation and then use the scientific method to the extent practical in applying the model in business.

Advantages in Using Hypotheses

A number of advantages result from the use of the hypothesis-testing approach in new product development, as outlined in Figure 10.17. Besides guiding the research process, as mentioned above, the disciplined thought process leads to the collection of *essential* information *only*, while assuring that all necessary aspects are covered. In researching new product opportunities there are many items of information that might be "interesting" but are not absolutely essential to the particular stage of the decision process. This is especially true in early phases of the investigation where one can become fascinated with details, such as whether the display should have green or red lights before it has been decided that a visual display will be needed. Without the necessary discipline, which stems from the hypothesis-testing process, the research can be overly exhaustive, overly consuming of valuable time, and overly expensive. Remember that the achievement of greater *efficiency* in the new product evaluation process is one of the major needs mentioned in Chapter 1 which we have attempted to answer with the procedures developed.

Using them:

1. Guides research process

2. Disciplines thought process and leads to collection of essential information only

3. Insures coverage of all relevant aspects (together with Planned Innovation model)

4. Helps preserve objectivity of all involved

5. Prevents misunderstandings—(situation usually shifts during research process)

6. Preserves reasoning process over time

7. Helps organize and relate diverse information to logical findings and conclusions

8. Helps organize report writing

FIGURE 10.17

Returning to Figure 10.17, items 4, 5, and 6 are closely related. The hypothesis statement and testing process helps preserve the objectivity of all persons or departments involved by reducing to writing the beliefs held at various stages of the research process. The reduction to writing prevents misunderstandings which almost invariably result because the state of knowledge changes over time. Remember that the time frame involved in new product developments is typically three to five years or longer. Key managers get promoted, and new personnel have no way to learn what the reasoning process was several years ago when the project was started. But even without shifts in personnel, as knowledge grows over time, viewpoints about the market need, technological alternatives, or competition almost unconsciously change. To keep the logical decision process on track, one needs to be able to look back to a year or two before and review just what the reasoning process was at the beginning, before the new information had begun coloring the situation. In preserving harmonious working relationships among the various departments involved (R&D, Marketing, Production) it is valuable to be able to review the original technical, marketing, competitive, and possibly manufacturing cost assumptions which led to the initiation of the project in the first place. What appears today to be an uneconomical approach or inadequate market size may have been perfectly logical three years before.

Finally, the hypothesis statement and testing process are of considerable benefit in organizing the diverse informational inputs and preparing research reports (items 7 and 8 in Figure 10.17). They also help provide a check that all pertinent information has indeed been obtained, and no more, as mentioned above.

Writing hypotheses is often considered an awkward chore when first learning the research process. The authors' experience has shown, however, that within a few weeks, personnel become skilled and comfortable with the task.

Before turning to specific research methods used in applying all the above procedures to industrial/commercial and consumer products, we must introduce one additional concept: that of elements of need, or buying motives. As we shall explain below, the *choice* of research technique depends on the mix of these elements.

Elements of Need Determine Research Procedures

We recognize today that both industrial and consumer buying behavior is a complex process. A number of scholars have developed rather sophisticated models of both processes.[1] Closely related to buying behavior are the bases of need, which have a major influence on the techniques used to determine the requirements for a new product. The need for any industrial or consumer product may be characterized as a mix of economic and emotive elements or buying motives. Techniques for analysis are also conditioned by the presence of multiple buying influences, which, although not unimportant for consumer goods, are especially important for certain classes of industrial goods, such as purchases of large capital equipment and installations.

Elements of Need

Every purchase, whether industrial or consumer, is based on a mixture of economic and emotive bases, or elements of need. The approximate mix of elements is shown in Figure 10.18. Note that the purchase of industrial/commercial products is based largely on economic elements; the mix is estimated to range from 90 percent economic (and 10 percent emotive) to 60 percent economic (and 40 percent emotive). For example, the mix of elements involved in the purchase of a new transfer-line for a gear and axle plant would probably be about 90 percent economic and 10 percent emotive. However, the purchase of furnishings for the plant manager's office would likely involve a mix of about 60 percent economic and 40 percent emotive.

Consumer purchases are believed normally to be based on a larger component of emotive elements than are industrial pro-

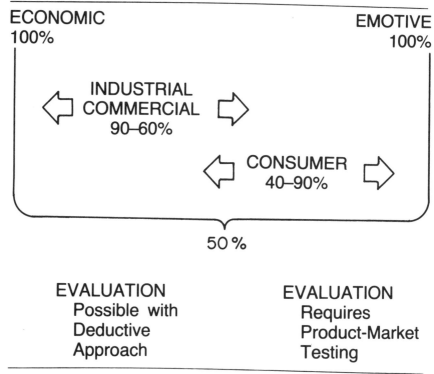

FIGURE 10.18 Basis of Need.

ducts. The mix here is estimated to range from 90 percent emotive (and 10 percent economic) to 40 percent emotive and 60 percent economic. Perhaps perfume comes closest to being purchased almost solely on emotive elements of need, but even in this case the mix is perhaps 90 percent emotive and 10 percent economic. A large purchase of a durable good such as an auto, a home, or a washing machine would probably involve a mix of elements more nearly 50 percent emotive and 50 percent economic.

The mix of elements of need is important in new product innovation, because the techniques for evaluating needs related to economic elements are different from those for evaluating needs related to emotive elements. As shown in Figure 10.18, a straightforward deductive research approach can be used when the bases are predominantly economic. On the other hand, when the bases are largely emotive, the research process requires a series of interactions with the consumer, from initial product concept to final product (and marketing mix) testing. The basic conceptual model of requirements for successful innovation presented above applies in both cases. However, different techniques are needed to evaluate the market requirements domain of the model for different mixes of economic and emotively based needs. Applications to both industrial/commercial and consumer products are explained in Chapters 11 and 12, respectively.

Multiple Buying Influences May Be Important As Well

We know that multiple buying influences exist for both consumer and industrial/commercial products. Multiple influences for consumer products can be taken into account to some extent in researching needs if the design of focus groups, concept tests, central location tests, in home tests, etc., can be made to include the major influences, i.e., persons involved. This may be possible where the major purchase influences are within the same household. For most consumer products, however, it is questionable whether the added effort and cost to evaluate multiple influences individually produces significantly greater insight than attempting to identify the major decision maker and dealing with that person alone.[2] This position is strengthened by the contention that a person making a major purchase affecting others in the household will attempt to integrate the needs and wants of others into his or her purchase decision.[3]

In dealing with industrial, commercial, or military products the situation is quite different. Where multiple influences exist, different persons can and should be sought out individually in order to understand the total elements of need. A committee may be involved in a major industrial purchase, such as a new computer. For example, in the construction industry the needs of distributors, contractors, and tradesmen, as well as final consumers, must be considered in the product design.

In serving military markets, the needs of different services and different commands within services, with different missions, must be considered in determining the requirements for a new product.

The task in evaluating multiple influences is usually straightforward, but time-consuming. The critical problem and potential source of misdirection lies in not correctly identifying the principal influences. Although the amount of field work can be extensive, the development cannot proceed with confidence of success unless the total need is understood and reflected in the product design. In the next chapter (11) we describe the research procedures appropriate for industrial/commercial products where economic buying elements predominate, and multiple buying influences are common. In Chapter 12 we present research methods appropriate when a large degree of emotive elements are present, as in consumer and some industrial/commercial products.

Summary

Requirements for successful new product innovation must be analyzed in five principal domains: (1) the marketing domain, (2) the physical requirements domain, (3) the resource requirements domain, (4) the economic requirements domain, and (5) the competitive requirements domain. The total requirement represents a simultaneous solution of the requirements in each of the five domains.

126

Investigation of requirements in each domain is facilitated by focusing on the intersections of the five domains while pursuing the answer to four framework questions:

1. How is the function performed now (for which the new product or service is expected to provide improvement)?
2. What does the present method cost?
3. What is wrong with the present method and what improvements are needed in present methods?
4. What value would the improvements have (to the intended user)?

The resulting matrix of information represents the total requirement for successful innovation.

The Bacon-Butler procedures represent an attempt to apply the scientific method to the field of new product innovation. The hypothesis formulation and testing procedure characteristic of other scientific techniques is found useful in new product evaluation as well. The choice among research techniques depends on the mix of economic and emotive elements of needs and on the existence of multiple buying influences.

Footnotes to Chapter 10

[1]See: Jagdish N. Sheth, "A Model of Industrial Buyer Behavior," *Journal of Marketing,* Vol. 37 (October 1973), pp. 50–56; and J. F. Engel, D. T. Kollat, and R. D. Blackwell, *Consumer Behavior* (New York: Holt Rinehart and Winston, Inc., 1968).

[2]I. C. M. Cunningham and R. R. Green, "Purchasing Decisions Roles in the U.S. Family, 1955 and 1973," *Journal of Marketing,* Vol. 38 (October 1974), pp. 61–64.

[3]Harry L. Davis, "Decision Making Within the Household," *Journal of Consumer Research,* Vol. 2 (March 1976), pp. 241–61.

Chapter 11

Research Procedures for Industrial/ Commercial Products

In the previous chapter we described the general research procedure and information needed to evaluate the new product opportunity regardless of the mix of need elements involved. In the present chapter we address that class of products where economic elements of need predominate in the purchase decision. Such is true of most products for industrial and commercial markets, as contrasted with those for consumer markets. The reader should be aware, however, that no products are purchased solely on economic motives. Some emotive component is always present. One of the key elements in the success of any new product innovation is the proper recognition of the mix of economic and emotive elements of demand.

A frequent cause of marginal success in new industrial/ commercial products is the failure to recognize a significant aspect of emotive demand. This was the case with early developments in electronic voice synthesis. Although the products apparently met all intelligibility requirements, the intangible (emotive) elements associated with the quality of a "robot-sounding" voice undoubtedly limited the early success of this major technical advancement. And some products for quasi-commercial markets such as the medical, health care, and military markets may have large components of emotive demand. This class of product is discussed in Chapter 12 where we deal with research procedures when significant emotive appeal is present.

Overview of Industrial/Commercial New Product Development Process

The suggested sequence of activities associated with the evaluation, development, and introduction of new industrial/

commercial products is shown in Figure 11.1. It is assumed that economic elements of demand predominate. Note that after passing the screening criteria, three stages of evaluative research—exploratory, qualitative, and quantitative—are performed prior to beginning technical development (step 5). Initial prototypes (step 6) are used for technical (as opposed to market) evaluation, followed by pilot production of prototypes for testing in the actual market environment (step 7). If buying motives are almost entirely economic, the focus of the pilot test is on meeting technical performance specifications. If significant emotive elements are also present, the pilot test phase may have to be expanded to evaluate these elements as thoroughly as possible. Upon completion of the pilot tests the production model is finalized (step 8), as are the marketing and production plans. This is followed by full-scale production and marketing efforts (step 9). The steps at which return on investment (ROI) analyses can be made is also shown in

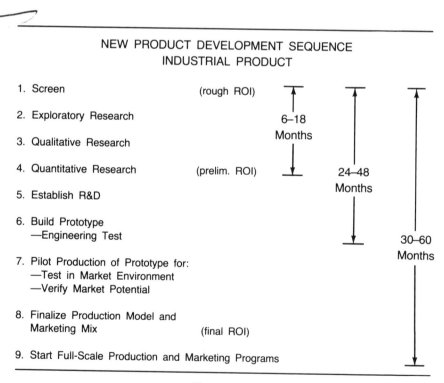

NEW PRODUCT DEVELOPMENT SEQUENCE
INDUSTRIAL PRODUCT

1. Screen (rough ROI)

2. Exploratory Research

6–18 Months

3. Qualitative Research

4. Quantitative Research (prelim. ROI)

24–48 Months

5. Establish R&D

6. Build Prototype
—Engineering Test

30–60 Months

7. Pilot Production of Prototype for:
—Test in Market Environment
—Verify Market Potential

8. Finalize Production Model and
Marketing Mix (final ROI)

9. Start Full-Scale Production and Marketing Programs

Figure 11.1

the figure, as well as the approximate total time required for major phases of activity.

The primary attention of the Bacon-Butler approach is centered on the first four steps in the process prior to technical development. Recall from discussions in Chapter 1 that the primary cause of new product failures is inadequate assessment of market requirements. Given a properly selected (screened) product opportunity, the key to successful development lies in proper evaluation and guidance. This is provided in steps 2, 3, and 4.

Three Research Steps Provide Greater Total Efficiency

Why should there be three steps instead of one combined effort? Because greater total efficiency is achieved. If for some reason the potential opportunity is unlikely to lead to success, it is important to detect the flaw quickly, with minimum expenditure. There is no need to completely document the requirements if it becomes obvious that the firm should not proceed with the development. The three-phase research procedure is therefore designed, first, to quickly detect (and reject) opportunities which clearly should not be pursued, even though they have passed the initial screening process. Second, the procedure is designed to clarify and define the requirements for success with increasing levels of research effort so that the new product development is guided and shaped toward ultimate success. Of course, it may become apparent at the second or even third state of the investigation that the requirements cannot be met, or that profits will not be adequate to justify continuing efforts.

This approach is consistent with scientific methodology, where hypotheses are established and then every effort is made to disqualify them, hoping, of course, that they will survive the test. But the approach goes much beyond mere testing for rejection. It has the more positive thrust of identifying the requirements and guiding the total development toward ultimate success if any possibility exists.

Exploratory Research Phase

The exploratory research phase is actually an extension of the screening process which preceded it. Its main purpose, as shown

131

in Figure 11.2, is to answer the fundamental question, "Why should this company (division) pursue this particular new product opportunity?" Implicit in this question are the questions of whether the opportunity meets the company objectives and provides a good matching of the particular company resources to the opportunity. These questions were, of course, addressed in the screening process, but now they will be evaluated in greater depth.

EXPLORATORY INVESTIGATION

PURPOSE:
To answer, "Why should this company (division) pursue this new product opportunity?"

FOCUS OF HYPOTHESES:
- Is there a market need?
- Is there a match of company (division) resources to opportunity?
  —Qualitative
  - Can the company handle the technology, production, marketing, financing?
  —Quantitative
  - Is the market large enough, or too large, to pass the screen?
- Is there a competitive opening? Why now?
- Check any doubtful aspect regarding passing the screening criteria

PROCEDURE:
- State hypotheses
- Select nonrandom sample
- Identify a few (6–10), knowledgeable, cooperative users (friends)
- Use nonstructured, personal interview, guided by hypotheses

OUTPUT:
- Does opportunity warrant further evaluation and meet screening criteria?

CONCLUSION:
- Decide whether to discontinue or establish priority for starting qualitative analysis

TIME AND EFFORT:
- 4 to 7 weeks, and 160 to 360 man-hours

Figure 11.2

Thus the main focus for the exploratory hypothesis is on three areas: first, "Is there really a market need, and why?" and second, "Is there really a good match qualitatively and quantitatively of our resources to the opportunity?" The third area of emphasis, also indicated in Figure 11.2, is the basis for competitive advantage. This can be pursued by addressing the question, "Why is there a competitive opening for us at this point in time?"

Additionally, if any doubtful aspects of the opportunity were disclosed during the screening process, these are flagged for additional investigation.

Exploratory Hypotheses

The procedure followed in the exploratory research phase is also outlined in Figure 11.2. Note at the bottom of the figure that time required is four to seven weeks with a manpower effort of 160 to 360 man-hours. The first step in the procedure is the framing of hypotheses. The basic requirements model (Figure 10.9) provides an outline for these hypotheses, while the three areas mentioned above provide emphasis. Hypotheses should be written concerning the four corners plus competition, starting with the upper left corner of the requirements model (the physical [and emotive] market need [requirements]).

Is There a Market Need?

One or more hypotheses should be written concerning why there is a market need and who, i.e., what specific segments, has the need. Hypotheses should be framed with a "because" statement. For example: "There is a need for improved automatic flight control of all types of commercial aircraft to permit all-weather "hands-off" landing at all major airports, *because* (1) the technology exists to do it; (2) the costs due to delays, wasted fuel, and lost revenues would easily pay for it; and (3) most major airlines would like to retrofit their aircraft in the near future if a reliable system were available." The value of the "because" statement cannot be overemphasized, because the reasons stated there provide immediate guidance for the investigation. In the above example, the research must verify (1) that the technology really exists, (2) that costs due to the factors mentioned would likely pay for such a system, within a particular time period, and (3) that most airlines are really anxious to retrofit existing equipment, and if so would specify how many of what type of aircraft would be involved and at what time. In a case like this, it would be appropriate to investigate what might delay adoption of the change, even if there were strong desire on the part of the airlines. Knowing the strong involvement of the Federal Aviation Administration (FAA) in certifying any aircraft guidance system, hypotheses regarding FAA approval and timing would be appropriate.

Is There A Match of Resources to the Opportunity?

Next, in framing the hypotheses, the upper-right corner of the requirements model is used for guidance. Here hypotheses regarding the technology to be involved in the design of the product are addressed. Again the "because" type of statement is valuable in guiding the subsequent investigation. We should also note here, that in framing hypotheses in all areas of the requirements model, ordinarily no one person is capable of doing it alone. And no one is expected to have all the answers. However, the research should start with the best input available from the most knowledgeable persons in the firm.

Therefore, in framing the hypotheses regarding technology to be involved, the director of engineering frequently must be involved, as may be several other key technical staff members. The necessity becomes even greater during the qualitative phase of research where more detailed hypotheses are necessary. At the exploratory stage, the technical hypotheses may center only on which of several technical approaches may be needed, given that the company is stronger in certain technologies than in others. Extending the above aircraft control example, the technical hypotheses may center on digital versus analog types of control technology, with associated reasons explaining why one or the other should or should not be more appropriate.

There may be a number of specific technical questions which need investigation. However, the researcher must avoid digging too deeply into technical issues at this stage in the investigation. Only those technical questions should be addressed which pertain to whether or not the firm has adequate technical capability (or can acquire it) to undertake the development.

Hypotheses regarding manufacture again should relate to whether or not the firm has the capability (or can acquire it) to produce the product within expected cost, performance, and testing requirements. The approximate volumes, techniques, and precision required in manufacture often provide the basis for the hypotheses which must be tested in this area.

Hypotheses regarding marketing and distribution methods often involve the geographic coverage, installation, service, and parts capability needed to compete effectively. When the firm already serves the market and is considering a new product for the same market, there may be no major questions which must be investigated in this area. However, if the market is new and unfamiliar, the question of adequacy of marketing resources and knowledge in this domain can be of central importance.

Moving to the lower-left corner of the basic requirements model (Figure 10.9), we address the questions of cost and value of the function. Hypotheses generally focus on the cost of present methods, if known, together with the possible additional value from the new approach being considered. It is important to identify the *reasons* different aspects of the need have certain value, such as indicated above regarding the value of better automated guidance and control equipment for commercial aircraft. For example, the value of improved maintenance service can be related to the cost of downtime of equipment. One or more hypotheses are appropriate concerning the value of benefits, with reasons "why" included in the "because" statements.

Is There a Competitive Opening? Why Now?

The final area for which hypotheses are needed concerns competition. Many firms charge blindly into new product opportunities feeling that they do not have to worry about competition initially, because they can figure out how to compete effectively when they "get a 'feel' for the new market." Yes, fools still rush in where wise men fear to tread. Yet the early identification of the probable basis of differential competitive advantage is not difficult and can be of tremendous value. Not only can it be a signal to abandon the development if no advantage can be foreseen; it can also provide guidance about what type of product features might be developed for selected market segments in order to be able to compete *profitably* from the beginning.

The key is to be able to *compete profitably from the beginning*. Often firms enter a market, find they cannot compete effectively, and then "slide sideways" into adjacent segments or begin to modify the product to be more competitive. Several years of unprofitable operation can result from this mode of introduction before the adjustments render adequate returns.

Exploratory hypotheses should be formulated to identify the basis of competitive advantage, such as improved technology, lower-cost manufacturing, and better installation and service. Furthermore, it is important to focus on *why* there is a competitive opening *now* and to identify what has created the "strategic window." Hypotheses should also be framed and tested regarding the significance to the customer of the anticipated competitive advantage. For example, if fast service response time is anticipated to be a major competitive advantage, the hypotheses should state why it *should* be an advantage to the customer (in terms of cost or benefit), and this should be tested in the exploratory investigation.

In summary, the principal focus of the exploratory hypothesis is (1) on verifying the existence of a real market need, (2) on assuring that the opportunity represents a good match of company resources to the opportunity (in terms of size of market, technology, production, and marketing capabilities), and (3) on insuring that an adequate basis for protection from competitive reaction exists before the new opportunity is pursued. The basic Bacon-Butler requirements model provides an outline of the various areas in which hypotheses must be framed in order to achieve the three-part focus. Now let us examine how the researcher proceeds to test the series of exploratory hypotheses.

Testing Exploratory Hypotheses

Information to test the hypothesis is obtained from knowledgeable cooperative users by means of personal interviews, as outlined in Figure 11.2. An attempt is made to identify six to ten friendly, cooperative potential customers who would be a user of the new product or who are intimately knowledgeable about the problem being solved by the new product. When the customer is a firm or institution, several people within the firm may have to be interviewed to get a complete understanding of the problem being solved, such as the aircraft control system problem mentioned above. (Thus, the number of interviews required within the 6–10 firms may total as many as 30 to 50.) If views are likely to differ among users or others who might influence the product design, such as the aircraft manufacturers or the FAA in the previous example, then several persons in those organizations should be interviewed as well. Again, the researcher must be highly selective when choosing persons to be interviewed to find those who are most knowledgeable (and cooperative) concerning the function in question.

No Need for Random Sample

There is no need to select a random sample at this stage of investigation. The attempt is to find those who understand the need, how it is being met now, and who are willing to discuss it openly. One may have to talk to several persons in the organization to find the appropriate persons. Often company salesmen or customers can provide leads to such persons. Typically, engineers and technical personnel are more knowledgeable and more likely to be cooperative than others in the organization.

The authors are often asked, "How do you know when you have found the right persons?" The answer lies in the *reasons* given to the questions asked. The interviewer must constantly ask "why" and evaluate the credibility of the source by the depth of knowledge displayed and the logic involved in the answers.

Hypotheses and Framework Questions Provide Structure for Interviews and Reports

Interviews need not be highly structured. The hypotheses, especially the "because" statements, provide an outline for the interview. Each hypothesis can be explored with the four framework questions shown previously in Figure 10.10. (1) How is it (automatic landing) done now? (2) What are the costs of doing it now (including cost of delays, lost bookings, etc.)? (3) What is wrong with the way it is done now and/or what improvement is needed? and (4) What would be the value of the improvements if the present problems or inadequacies were overcome?

Note that the same four framework questions can be used to explore (test) hypotheses concerning market need, technical design, manufacturing, marketing, and competition. Thus, logical, organized interviews can be conducted without a formal questionnaire if the hypotheses have been committed to memory. At most, a few notes concerning the hypotheses are all that is needed to guide the interview.

During the interview a few notes need to be taken concerning each hypothesis. After the interview is concluded, the researcher can summarize the information relative to each hypothesis in a trip report format. The trip reports can be circulated to others within the company to keep them advised of the progress of the investigation while it proceeds.

When the entire series of interviews is completed, the information from different sources can be aggregated and summarized according to each hypothesis tested. The conclusion regarding the tests of various hypotheses can then be further summarized according to the three major areas of focus described above: (1) Is there really a market need? (2) Is there a good match of the company resources to this opportunity? and (3) Is there a competitive opening?

If there are no major negative findings in these areas, the logical overall conclusion is to proceed with the next phase of investigation, the qualitative analysis. Any major negative finding would dictate terminating the investigation at this point.

Conclusion From Research

The reader may wonder how a conclusive test of the hypotheses can be made with interviews at only six to ten firms. The answer is first that only a negative conclusion, to discontinue the project, is final. And that conclusion may be final only for the time being. Once any major negative factor is discovered (such as inadequate market demand or inadequate resources to undertake the development), there is no need for further research. The project should be halted until the negative factor is eliminated, possibly merely by the passage of time or by acquisition of needed resources.

Secondly, let us consider what we mean by a negative conclusion. In the case of new product developments, we consider the "absence of decidedly positive results" to be "negative" results. In view of the many risks and uncertainties surrounding any new product venture, the authors' experience has shown that the development should not proceed unless all the signals (in the three areas mentioned) are positive.

For example, in exploring the need for a new approach to a function such as the automatic aircraft landing control mentioned above, unless the persons or firms likely to benefit most by the new development are enthusiastic about the possible development, their attitude should be considered a negative factor. A potentially successful new product will be met by comments like, "I never thought of that, but it is a real problem, and, we'd like to see you come up with a better solution." Likewise, a good match of resources will be greeted by comments like, "Yes, I can see why it would make sense for your firm to be entering that area; you certainly are the leader in that general field." The general field might be automatic guidance and control for military aircraft. On the other hand, a potential mismatch of resources to opportunities will be met by sincere comments (if the persons are genuinely cooperative) such as, "Well, that's a real problem, but I can't see how your firm with no previous experience in that technology (or no previous relevant manufacturing or marketing experience) could really be successful, given the competition you will eventually have to face."

The third reason why six to ten firms normally suffice is that a positive decision to proceed does not mean conclusive endorsement of the project. A positive conclusion means only that the opportunity warrants further, more extensive analysis. Thus the reader can see why we termed the exploratory phase an extension of the screening process. The thrust of the effort is to more selectively weed out those opportunities which have substantial shortcomings even though they passed the initial screening process. Again, efficiency with the new product development process is greatly enhanced by expending major efforts *only* on products which are going to succeed. And, typically, five to ten unsuccessful exploratory investigations are done before finding one opportunity which justifies the qualitative research. Of course, if several opportunities pass the exploratory phase, priorities for proceeding to the qualitative phase may have to be established, depending on the resources available for the qualitative research.

Qualitative Research Phase

Called by many users the "heart" of the Bacon-Butler approach, the qualitative research phase is the stage where the new product requirements are identified and documented to guide subsequent development efforts. Although products may be rejected at the conclusion of this phase, the major thrust is the positive identification of requirements leading to later success.

The qualitative phase has three major purposes as outlined in Figure 11.3. These are (1) to determine the range of variation in product requirements (physical, technical, and economic) needed for different market segments; (2) to determine the range of resource requirements needed (R&D, production, marketing, financial) to exploit the opportunity; and (3) to identify the competitors, including especially their strengths and weaknesses and the characteristics of their products.

Qualitative Hypotheses

Qualitative hypotheses focus the research on identifying the *range of variation* in requirements. The most important variations are typically found in physical and economic requirements. For example, to meet the needs in some market segments, a new electronic computer may require a small memory, relatively slow central processing unit (CPU), and slow printer, whereas other segments require larger memories, and faster CPU and printer speeds. Similarly, one market segment may have little displaceable clerical cost, whereas other segments may have large amounts on which to justify the investment in such a computer.

Large variations in physical and economic requirements are often paralleled by variations in technical and production requirements. The slower, lower-cost machine may be able to use a simpler, lower-cost technology, involving state-of-the-art production methods and materials, without the need for special designs and materials, new processes, or tight quality control, compared to that needed for the larger and faster machine. Furthermore, large variations in physical, economic, technical, and production requirements often signal similar variation in financial and marketing resources needed to serve the range of market segments. Thus, requirements in all areas must be addressed, although the most critical differences may be reflected in the physical and economic requirements.

The nature and role of qualitative hypotheses can perhaps best be understood by exploring how qualitative hypotheses differ from exploratory hypotheses. In summary, the difference lies in the level of detail, which, in turn, reflects the difference in purpose between the two research phases. Exploratory hypotheses

QUALITATIVE ANALYSIS

PURPOSE:
- To determine range of variation in product requirements:
  —Physical
  —Technical
  —Economic
- To determine range of resource requirements:
  —Production
  —Marketing
  —Financial
- To identify competitors and characteristics of competitive products

FOCUS OF HYPOTHESES:
- To identify requirements: (Range)
  —Physical
  —Technical
  —Economic
  —Production
  —Marketing
  —Financial

PROCEDURE:
- Select (nonrandom) sample of users to represent range of variation in requirements
- Use prestructured questionnaire
- Use personal interview
- May require interviews at several levels in organization

OUTPUT:
- Identification of Requirements
- Conclusion:
  Product requirements are (are not) feasible for company to meet (technical, production, marketing, economic)
- Conclusion:
  There is (is not) a reasonable basis for competitive advantage

CONCLUSION:
- Discontinue or continue with quantitative analysis

TIME AND EFFORT:
- 10 to 20 weeks, and 500 to 2000 man-hours

Figure 11.3

tend to be broad and general statements because their purpose is likewise broad and general. Exploratory hypotheses regarding physical and technical requirements are intended merely to assure that a reasonable match of resources to opportunity will be possible if the new venture is undertaken. Qualitative hypotheses, on the other hand, must guide the investigation toward identifying the operational (physical) and technical requirements *in sufficient detail* to provide meaningful direction for the subsequent R&D effort.

Of course, exploratory hypotheses can be, and sometimes are, specified in greater detail than is necessary to reach their limited objective. If this is done, it often leads to one of two problems. First, if the project is discontinued after the exploratory phase, the extra degree of detail has added unnecessary expense to the total product development process. Second, if the project passes the exploratory stage, there is a tendency to continue into a "quasi-qualitative" stage without reformulating the hypotheses to the greater degree of specificity required to properly guide the qualitative phase. The tendency is to continue with the exploratory hypotheses providing guidance for the quasi-qualitative phase. This almost always leads to an inadequate qualitative investigation.

Because of the greater level of detail required, a larger number of hypotheses is generally needed for the qualitative phase in comparison to the exploratory phase. For example, in studying the possibility of entering the market for cultured marble vanity tops, Donnelly Mirrors, Inc. reduced the exploratory hypotheses with primary significance to the four shown in Figure 11.4.

However, when proceeding to the qualitative phase, the number of hypotheses was expanded to sixteen, each of which had several sub-parts. For example, the first of the four exploratory hypotheses shown above was expanded to the following more specific qualitative hypotheses shown in Figure 11.5. The remaining qualitative hypotheses covered other aspects of the total requirement. At this stage in the development of the methodology, the hypotheses were not organized according to the corners of the Bacon-Butler model of requirements discussed earlier, although examination of the hypotheses in the case will show that all aspects are covered.

To assure adequate coverage of every aspect, we now recommend classifying and grouping hypotheses according to the

1. DMI should enter the market for cultured marble because there is a need for a manufacturer who can produce cultured marble more efficiently and with more consistent quality.

2. Cultured marble is not in danger of being outmoded by another material.

3. The consumer demand for marble look-alikes, i.e., cultured marble, is increasing, especially in California.

4. There is no large manufacturer of cultured marble; most are small job shops.

Note: Presented with cooperation and permission of Donnelly Mirrors, Inc., Holland, Michigan.

Figure 11.4

corner segments of the requirements model, i.e., physical, economic, technical, manufacturing, marketing, and competitive.

Testing Qualitative Hypotheses

An outline of the procedures used and the time and effort required (10 to 20 weeks and 500 to 2000 man-hours) in the qualitative investigation is also presented in Figure 11.3. The first step is to select a sample (normally of customers or users) which represents the range of variation in the target market segments to be examined. This need not be a statistically random sample, because it is not intended to be an accurate reflection of the size of markets in each segment. It is chosen to represent the full range of differences expected in all aspects of requirements—physical, economic, technical, etc.—although the principal differences usually show up in the physical and economic requirements, as discussed earlier.

For example, when studying the requirements for automatic labor-time recording in manufacturing plants, the range or requirements depended mainly on the number of employees, the type of pay system (straight hourly, piece rate, incentives, etc.), the variations in product manufactured, and the associated method of

143

1. Donnelly should enter the synthetic marble market because:
   A. There is a need for another supplier because existing manufacturers cannot produce a product:
      1) That is uniform in color.
      2) Efficiently.
         a. Costs are high.
         b. Delivery time is poor.
   B. Donnelly has a new process that will enable them to produce a product:
      1) That is uniform in color.
      2) More efficiently.
         a. At lower costs.
         b. With better delivery time.
2. Uniformity in color between batches is important because:
   A. At the point of purchase, color irregularity causes the customer to think the product lacks quality.
   B. The products are often sold in sets that must match in color.
   C. Products are made and carried in inventory instead of produced to order, which means a given set may not be all from the same batch.
3. Uniformity in color between batches is not as important if:
   A. A set is special-ordered because the whole set will be made from one batch.
4. Standard-size products are important because:
   A. It would be inefficient to make synthetic marbles by means of batch processing.
   B. It is important to have readily available inventories to satisfy the spread necessary to obtain an order.
   C. Many counters, vanities, walls, toilets, etc., that a marble product would be attached to, are of standard size.
5. Flexibility (quick changes with little waste) in the process for manufacturing synthetic marble products is important because:
   A. Special orders may come in at any time.
   B. Special orders may be small in volume of material required.
   C. This will increase the efficiency by eliminating waste associated with batch processing.
6. Small, back-alley manufacturers of synthetic marble products are inefficient because:
   A. They are poorly managed.
   B. They use inefficient processes.
   C. They do not have economies of scale.

Note: Presented with cooperation and permission of Donnelly Mirrors, Inc., Holland, Michigan.

Figure 11.5

manufacture (job shop, batch, assembly line, etc.). Thus, a small plant producing a standard product with a few models mainly for inventory with similar (standard) assembly procedures would normally pay its employees on a straight hourly basis, possibly with some group incentive. There would be no need to relate the individual wage to individual piece parts produced because a simple standard cost accounting system would be adequate for control. This would be an example of the simplest physical and economic requirement.

At the opposite end of the spectrum might be a large producer of special capital equipment. In this case a large variety of products is produced to order. Job-shop production methods would normally be used with records required of actual (individual) labor time and cost on each operation in the entire manufacturing and assembly process. Some plants of this type employ complex incentive systems as well. The physical requirement to capture the labor time is much more extensive, and the value to the user of a successful system is far greater than for the simpler case first described. The reason for the greater value in the latter case is first, that a large number of time keepers must be presently employed to do the job. Secondly, and perhaps more importantly, effective cost control, inventory control, production control, and scheduling (i.e., manufacturing efficiency) are intimately related to the labor-time recording function, which not only captures the labor time and costs, but also the part numbers and processes completed. Thus, an effective labor-time recording system in this environment is the key to greater total efficiency in manufacturing as well as savings in time keeper labor.

These cases represent typical extremes in labor-time recording requirements. A typical middle case might involve a medium-sized producer of a mix of standard and special products. A job cost accounting system might not be required because a standard cost system with straight hourly payroll is workable. However, a large mix of standard and special products, with possibly different lot sizes, could produce significant production control and scheduling problems. In this case, if an efficient system were not in place, the labor-time recording system might be used to input the needed production data. And if a system were already in place, the labor-time recording system might be more efficient than that existing. Thus, the requirements for the new system would be more complex than the simplest case described, and the value greater as well. However, the requirements and value would be less than that of the large and complex job shop situation described.

In researching a product requirement such as this, it is necessary to study several cases of each type in the major target market segments of interest. Different segments must be investigated to assure that any variation among segments is understood.

Sample Size Required

Experience with a wide variety of industrial-commercial products has shown that the variations due to size and type of users can usually be adequately represented with a total sample size of 15 to 30 firms. A successful approach with the qualitative research has been first to identify the extremes in requirements and attempt to understand what causes the requirements to vary, as illustrated with the labor-time recording example above. Then additional cases can be selected on a logical basis. Usually the exploratory research will provide good insights of this nature to guide the initial qualitative interviews. After that, the deeper understanding which results from the first few qualitative interviews is used to guide the next series of investigations. The qualitative phase is terminated when the additional interviews are no longer disclosing major variations. But we have not discussed how all this information is obtained. Let us now consider that.

Data Collection Process for Qualitative Phase

Earlier, in Figure 10.16, we showed that our basic sequence starts with the model of requirements. It then proceeds to the hypotheses, then to the information needed to test the hypotheses, then to the questionnaire design needed to obtain the information, and finally to the actual collection of data. Presuming that we have specified the qualitative hypotheses, we must now determine what information is needed to test them. One might wonder, "Why not proceed directly to the questionnaire design?" There are two reasons. First, there may be information which will not be obtained via the questionnaire. This is usually the case for background data which may be available from publications, and for

146

technical information, which may require experimental analysis. This does not mean that the R&D program to develop the new product starts at this point. However, if there are questions concerning the technical feasibility of different approaches to the design, these may have to be addressed as part of the qualitative phase of investigation.

The second reason for not proceeding directly from hypotheses to questionnaire design hinges on the amount of information required, how it is interrelated, and what is needed. When studying a complex new product requirement such as a machine tool, a computer, or a weapons delivery system, an enormous amount of information will be needed, and the researcher must call on other specialists for assistance to assure that the correct information is obtained.

The questionnaire must then be constructed to follow a logical topical sequence for purposes of the interview, which usually is not the sequence needed for analysis. Question 1 in the interview may refer to hypotheses 3, 6, and 8; question 2 to hypotheses 1 and 5; etc.

Need for Prestructured Questionnaire

Another major difference between the exploratory and qualitative phases of research surfaces when we consider questionnaire design. Because of the volume and level of detail required in the qualitative phase, a careful prestructuring of the questionnaire is essential. This means the researcher must determine precisely what information must be obtained and from whom. And the terminology used and data requested must be in the normal language and format used by the respondent.

In order to get the most accurate and reliable information, it is necessary to obtain each item from the person best qualified to answer. For some items this may be the general manager of a plant; for others it may be a machine operator on the production floor. In studying the requirements for a computer system for small manufacturing firms, ten functional sub-areas were defined and examined for each firm studied.[1] These included (1) order processing and billing, (2) accounts receivable, (3) purchasing and accounts payable, (4) production control and scheduling, (5) raw material and purchased parts inventory control, (6) finished goods inventory control, (7) payroll, (8) cost accounting, (9) sales analysis, and (10) general accounting. Information needed for each area was first specified and a prestructured series of questions was designed for each one. The interview was started by explaining the purpose of the study to the president or general manager and asking three or four general questions. Then the interviewer asked, "May I speak to the person who handles your order processing and billing?" After asking a short series of questions, the interviewer asked to see the person handling accounts receivable, then purchasing and accounts payable, etc.

By grouping the questions by functional area and prestructuring the questions within each area, an enormous amount of accurate information can be obtained within a relatively short time. Furthermore, no one person within the firm is made to feel as though he or she has been imposed upon. In the case just mentioned, the data processing requirements for the firms were completely documented within 1½ to 2½ hours using an eleven-page prestructured questionnaire. Yet no single person within the firm had to spend more than 10 to 20 minutes with the interviewer. An example of one section of such a prestructured questionnaire used for the *payroll* function is included in Table 11-1 (pp. 150–51). As can be seen, the format was also precoded to simplify keypunching the data for computer analysis.

A section of the qualitative questionnaire used by Toledo Scale to determine the requirement for its product line which automatically counts parts by electronically weighing them is shown in Figure 11.6. In this case the form was not precoded for keypunching. The equipment which resulted from this research was shown previously in Figure 10.3.

In summary, the key to obtaining the amount and quality of information needed to test qualitative hypotheses (and to determine the product requirements) is to prestructure the questionnaire for ease in answering and to obtain the information from those persons who are most knowledgeable about individual aspects of the total requirements. Thus, although a sample size of 15 to 30 firms is usually adequate, there may be 5 to 10 short interviews with different individuals within each firm.

It should also be kept in mind that not all aspects of the requirements need to be specified in the same degree of detail. As was the case with exploratory hypotheses, only one or two areas usually require detailed investigation. Often the financial, pro-

PORTION OF QUALITATIVE QUESTIONNAIRE FOR
ELECTRONIC PARTS-COUNTING SCALES

I. Parts Characteristics
   1. How many different types of parts are counted in your department? _____
   2. How do you classify lot size?
      a. _____ Box
      b. _____ Case
      c. _____ Pallet
      d. _____ Loose Parts
      e. _____ Other
   3. What is the weight range for these parts?
      Minimum part weight _____ Avg. variance _____
      Maximum part weight _____ Avg. variance _____
      Average part weight _____ Avg. variance _____
   4. How are the variances in parts determined?
      a. _____ Absolute count
      b. _____ Random sampling
      c. _____ Estimation
      d. _____ Other (specify) _____
   5. What is the weight range for each lot size?
      Minimum lot weight _____ Number per lot _____
      Maximum lot weight _____ Number per lot _____
      Average lot weight _____ Number per lot _____
   6. What is the tare weight per lot in #5?
      Minimum tare weight _____
      Maximum tare weight _____
      Average tare weight _____
   7. What is the physical size of the lot?

	Physical Dimension in Inches		
	Length	Width	Depth
Minimum lot	_____	_____	_____
Maximum lot	_____	_____	_____
Average lot	_____	_____	_____

Note: Presented with the cooperation and permission of Toledo Scale Division, Reliance Electric Company, Worthington, Ohio.

Figure 11.6

duction, and marketing requirements are not significantly different from those for existing products. However, the analysis of competition is always important.

Analysis of Competition

If there were a law for new product development like the Peter Principle or Murphy's Law, it would surely be, "You can't

TABLE 11-1

PRESTRUCTURED QUALITATIVE QUESTIONNAIRE TO DETERMINE DATA PROCESSING REQUIREMENTS FOR PAYROLL FUNCTION

RECORD QUESTIONS a THROUGH e IN GRID BELOW

a. Normally, how many people does the company employ in the following categories? What is the maximum number? (READ LIST).
b. How are these groups paid? By salary, hourly rate, incentive pay, or commission, or combination?
c. Are they paid by cash or check?
d. What is the payroll period for each group?
e. How is attendance recorded for payroll?

Employee Categories

	Total	Admin. Exec. & Superv.	Clerical	Production	Maintenance	Engin. & Technical	Sales	Other
a. No. in Group	8,9,10	18,19	26,27	34,35,36	44,45	52,53	60,61	68,69
Average	11,12,13	20,21	28,29	37,38,39	46,47	54,55	62,63	70,71
Maximum								

b. *Type of Payroll* (circle)

Straight Salary	14-1	22-1	30-1	40-1	48-1	56-1	64-1	72-1
Hourly	-2	-2	-2	-2	-2	-2	-2	-2
Incentive	-3	-3	-3	-3	-3	-3	-3	-3
Hourly & Incentive	-4	-4	-4	-4	-4	-4	-4	-4
Straight Commission	-5	-5	-5	-5	-5	-5	-5	-5
Salary & Commission	-6	-6	-6	-6	-6	-6	-6	-6
	-X	-X	-X	-X	-X	-X	-X	-X

c. *Method of Payment*

Cash	15-1	23-1	31-1	41-1	49-1	57-1	65-1	73-1
Check	-2	-2	-2	-2	-2	-2	-2	-2
	-X	-X	-X	-X	-X	-X	-X	-X

d. *Payroll Period*

Day	16-1	24-1	32-1	42-1	50-1	58-1	66-1	74-1
Week	-2	-2	-2	-2	-2	-2	-2	-2
Two Weeks	-3	-3	-3	-3	-3	-3	-3	-3
Month	-4	-4	-4	-4	-4	-4	-4	-4
Other	-5	-5	-5	-5	-5	-5	-5	-5
(Specify)	-X	-X	-X	-X	-X	-X	-X	-X

e. *Attendance Record*

None Kept	17-1	25-1	33-1	43-1	51-1	59-1	67-1	75-1
Time Clock	-2	-2	-2	-2	-2	-2	-2	-2
Other	-3	-3	-3	-3	-3	-3	-3	-3
(Specify)	-X	-X	-X	-X	-X	-X	-X	-X

learn too much about your competition." Firms always tend to err in the direction of knowing *too little* about their competition. In many cases there seems to be a subconscious aversion to finding out about competitors and their products. That is one of the most important tasks during the qualitative phase. It is essential that the strengths and weaknesses of existing competitive products be thoroughly understood. Thus an analysis must be made of the characteristics of all major competing products. This can often be done by collecting sales literature and other published information. Present users of competing equipment are usually glad to explain and demonstrate its strong and weak points. They tend to be somewhat biased toward positive attributes, however, as we mentioned earlier, because they tend to defend their purchase decision. Users who are having difficulty with competing equipment are usually very vocal about their problems.

Users are also excellent sources of information concerning price as well as sales and service support provided by competitors for their products. In general, answers to the question, "What is wrong with existing (competing) equipment?" are a valuable source of information concerning ways to improve and differentiate the new product.

Almost always competitors are strong in certain aspects and weak in others. In addition to examining the characteristics of competitive products, it is important to evaluate their matching of resources to the opportunity. This means taking a broad view of their objectives and capabilities. Of course, the amount of information is not as complete as for your own firm, but a great deal of it is readily available without resorting to illegal covert activities. For example, valuable information is contained in annual reports, in reports prepared by stock brokerage firms, and from D&B reports. Additional information can be obtained by talking to users. Often competing salesmen will tell their customers of plans to introduce new equipment or to delete certain models. Trade shows are also a convenient, excellent source of information on competitive equipment. In short, every available legal source should be used.

When entering new markets for the first time, the competitive analysis can be a major task. In this case it is important to identify where the strongest competition will lie. For example, divisions of large corporations often are not as fierce competitors as are small or medium-sized firms whose whole future depends on a narrow product line. Just because a division of a powerful firm is in the market does not indicate the importance of that market or product line to the parent firm. If the direction of emphasis for the parent corporation has shifted, they may even be willing to sell the division.

Just such a situation was encountered within the past few years in studying the requirements for golf cars for AMF. One manufacturer of a quality golf car was found to be owned by a large firm in the insulation and building materials field. In view of the large potential in its primary field, it did not made sense that the large firm would devote resources to the highly competitive golf car field. It therefore came as no surprise when the corporation divested the golf car division a few months after the analysis had been made.

Output from Qualitative Analysis

In summary, the qualitative analysis should identify the range of variation of product and resource requirements needed to serve the intended target market segments. It should also provide an assessment of competition and characteristics of major competing products.

A significant level of detail must be reached by the analysis to clearly determine whether it is technically feasible to design and manufacture the range of products required within the economic constraints found and the resources of the firm. The analysis must also specify the physical, economic, and technical requirements in sufficient detail to be able to guide the R&D effort which may be initiated at the conclusion of the quantitative phase. The R&D effort cannot be initiated at the end of the qualitative phase because it will not have been determined which of the various possible product variations should be developed. The output of the quantitative phase is needed to complete this determination.

The qualitative analysis must also indicate whether the financial, production, marketing, and management resources are adequate to compete effectively in some or all of the market segments investigated. A clear competitive opening must be identified as well as the possible basis for continued protection from competitive reaction.

If it appears feasible to develop some or all of the product variations and to compete effectively in some or all of the market segments, the conclusion would be to continue with the quantitative analysis. Otherwise, the project would be discontinued, either permanently or temporarily, depending on the nature of the situation. Often projects which do not proceed immediately to the quantitative phase are put on the shelf to await a specified technological advancement, such as the availability of lower-cost computer memories. When the technical advancement occurs the project is reactivated and reviewed for any changes which might have occurred in the interim. Then the quantitative phase is initiated.

A Great Temptation

After the successful completion of a qualitative study, so much information is known about the product, the market, the resource requirements, and the competition that there is a great temptation to proceed immediately with the development. We have observed several such cases where the temptation was overwhelming to the company. In every case the economic consequences were undesirable: either outright disaster or much less profit than could have been obtained. The reason is that the qualitative research can be very *misleading* about the relative profit potential of different market segments. The qualitative survey is purposely biased to expose the range of possible variation to be faced. What is still needed is an *unbiased* assessment of the size of each market segment and the degree of competitive penetration in each. Both factors have a major impact on the ultimate profit to be realized. Thus, further technical development activity is not justified until the quantitative phase is completed, as we show in the next section.

Quantitative Research Phase

The quantitative research phase has two purposes, as mentioned above, and is shown in Figure 11.7. They are: (1) to measure the size of the market potential in various segments which correspond to major design variations in the product, and (2) to measure the extent of competitive penetration within each major segment. This phase is relatively simple and straightforward com-

PURPOSE:
- To determine market potential for major design variations in product
- To assess existing competitive market penetration

FOCUS OF HYPOTHESES:
- Differences of requirements for various market segments
- Size of various market segments (which have different requirements)
- Existence of competitive equipment in each market segment

PROCEDURE:
- Select random sample (statistical)
- Stratified by industry or other market segment
- Short pre-structured questionnaire containing minimum key information on quantity usages, sizes, costs, materials, competitive products used
- Telephone interview will usually suffice

OUTPUT:
- Size of market segments (potential) for different product variations
- Penetration of competition in each market segment

CONCLUSION:
- Discontinue or proceed with product design and development

TIME AND EFFORT:
- 8 to 12 weeks, and 320 to 960 man-hours

Figure 11.7

pared with the qualitative phase. The time required to complete the research is normally only 25 to 50 percent of that required for the qualitative phase.

If this is true, one may wonder why the phase is not conducted earlier, perhaps in parallel with the qualitative phase. The reason is that the output of the qualitative phase is necessary to design the quantitative phase. The basis for market segmentation and differences in equipment configuration needed for each segment are a principal output of the preceding qualitative phase. Also, the competitors and characteristics of their equipment,

155

identified in the previous phase, are needed to structure the quantitative research.

Quantitative Research Hypotheses

The framing of the quantitative research hypotheses is straightforward. As indicated in Figure 11.7, the hypotheses state that various market segments will represent major, moderate, or minor potential for certain reasons. The reasons normally relate (a) to combinations and strengths of the need-elements and (b) to the number of firms believed to have the characteristics. For example, the firms having the greatest need for automatic labor-time recording may be large firms producing special capital equipment, because the economic benefit will be so great. The main questions to be resolved may be (1) Is it possible to make a general system to handle the diverse requirements of such firms? and (2) Are there enough firms that have this strong need to justify entering this segment of the market. Another hypothesis might be that the firms producing a mix of standard and special parts on a quasi-assembly line basis can achieve moderate benefits from such a new system, and it is believed that there are many more such firms than large job shops. Thus, it might be much more profitable to develop a less sophisticated system for this larger market than tackle the more complex requirements of a smaller segment.

Identify Competitive Penetration

Hypotheses also should be developed regarding which segments competition has already penetrated, and why. The hypothesis may center on the belief that competition is strong in the segments with simple requirements because competing firms have been historically active in those markets and have excellent in-place service capabilities to serve those portions, but not others. Or the hypothesis may be that the technical sophistication demonstrated by competitive equipment may be grossly inadequate to meet requirements of other segments; thus they have very little penetration into those segments.

The number of individual segments which need investigation is determined by the number of hypotheses concerning important differences in need among the segments. Among industrial/com-

156

mercial products, needs often are different among certain industries and sizes of firm within industries. These dimensions thus often provide the basis for segmentation, which we discuss further in the section below.

Procedures for Testing Quantitative Hypotheses

An outline of the procedures, output, and conclusion from the test of quantitative hypotheses is summarized in Figure 11.7. The time required is about 8 to 12 weeks with an effort of approximately 320 to 960 man-hours, much of which may be contracted to an outside market research firm, if desired. The two key elements in the procedure are (1) the use of a stratified random (statistical) sample, and (2) the use of a short prestructured questionnaire usually administered by telephone.

Design of a Stratified Random Sample

In order to understand how (and why) the stratified random sample is constructed, let us first consider why a sample is used in the first place, why it should be random, and finally why it should be stratified.

A sample is used when it is impractical to survey the entire population in the target market segments. For industrial/commercial markets, the number of firms or institutions in the population can number in the thousands. On the other hand, when developing products for military markets, the branches of the services (Navy, Air Force, etc.) and sub-units involved may range from less than 6 to as many as 30. Thus, in many instances, when developing products for these markets, it is possible to survey every unit in the target market. That is not the typical case, however, for industrial/commercial or consumer markets with much larger populations.

The answer to the second issue, why the sample should be random has already been mentioned above. A random sample refers to the *process* by which the sample is drawn. The statistically random sampling process assures that every element in the population has a known probability of being chosen (usually an equal probability within a stratum) and that the selection of any one element does not affect the probability of selecting any other. In short, the sample is an unbiased representation of the population.

By way of contrast, recall that in selecting the qualitative sample, the process used is to select firms which are believed to have certain characteristics of special interest regarding the design of the new product. Once firms with certain characteristics have been selected and studied (such as small firms which pay only straight hourly wages), no more firms of that type are selected despite the possible fact that most firms may have those same characteristics. We move on to purposely select firms with other characteristics (such as large firms which pay on a piece-rate basis). When all the firms in the sample are gathered together, they represent what we want at that stage, the range of variation in requirements, but this sample almost certainly does not represent *proportionately* the characteristics of firms in the total population. The sample has been biased (purposely) by the selection process.

Returning to the quantitative sample, why choose a stratified random sample? Stratification is used for greater efficiency in the sampling process. If every firm in the population had basically the same characteristics of interest (size, wage payment plan, method of production, etc.), it would not be necessary to stratify the sample. A simple random sample consisting of one respondent would suffice.

On the other hand, where there are a number of significant variations in the population which affect the new product requirements, each of these variations must be proportionately represented in the sample so that estimates of the similar population proportions can be made with a suitable level of statistical precision. To do this with one simple random sample would require a huge sample size compared to a stratified sample, which gives the same overall statistical precision. Moreover, the critical statistical estimates usually involve the size of certain individual market segments and the degree of competition penetration within the segments.

Thus the selection of sample strata hinges (1) on the significant variations among market segments, and (2) the expected degree of competition within each of them, all of which were or should have been identified in the qualitative phase of research.

For example, in studying the requirements for an automatic weighing and labeling machine to be used in supermarkets and large grocery stores for weighing prepackaged meat such as hamburger and pork chops, the following stratification was used. Equipment configurations were expected to vary according to meat volumes handled, and competitive penetration was expected to be greater in certain types of stores, e.g., independents, chains, cooperatives, etc. It was also expected to be related to the size of the store. It was thus decided that a three-by-three stratification according to these criteria was necessary as shown below.

STORE TYPE

	Independent	Chain	Cooperative
Large	1	4	7
Medium	2	5	8
Small	3	6	9

As a result, the sample size required depended mainly on the degree of statistical precision needed in any one of the nine individual cells. In this case, it was decided that equal precision was desired in each cell.

Level of Statistical Precision Required

Based on experience with this type of research in commercial/industrial environments, a practical decision criterion for resulting confidence interval estimates is ± 10 percent error at the 90 percent level of confidence for the smallest individual cell. Thus, when cells are aggregated (such as for all independent stores, large, medium-sized, and small), the resulting error in estimates would be much less. In most scientific research a criterion of ± 5 percent at the 95 percent level of confidence is the accepted norm. However, in view of the other large sources of error in conducting field research in the industrial/commercial market environment, it is generally accepted that the scientific norm is not economically appropriate, because it would require a considerably larger sample.

A simple technique for estimating the size of the sample needed within an individual cell is as follows. Presume that the critical estimates will be binominal in nature, such as the percentage of small independent stores which presently use competitive equipment. The worst case for statistical estimation would occur when 50 percent of the stores did and 50 percent did not.

159

This could be used as a design criterion, or perhaps a more optimistic 70 percent vs. 30 percent split. Presuming that the firm is sampling from a large enough population of stores so that the resulting sample size will not exceed 10 percent of the population size, the following formula can be used to estimate the sample size needed:[2]

$$n = \frac{z^2 pq}{e^2}$$

where

n = sample size

z = standard normal error (for 90% level of confidence, z = 1.96; for 90% level of confidence, z = 1.645)

p = proportion in population expected to have attribute in question, i.e., 50% = .5

q = 1 − p

e = error in confidence interval estimate expressed in decimal form: e.g., 5% = .05; 10% = .10

Thus, the sample size required for ± 10 percent error at 90 percent level of confidence where 50 percent of the population has an attribute and 50 percent does not would be calculated as follows:

$$n = \frac{(1.645)^2 \times (.5)(.5)}{(.1)^2} = \frac{(2.706) \times (.25)}{.01} = 67$$

Rather than design for the worst case, if it is presumed that the population will never be divided more than .7 to .3 on any issue, the sample size required would be as follows:

$$n = \frac{(1.645)^2 \times (.7)(.3)}{(.1)^2} = \frac{(2.706) \times (.21)}{.01} = 56.8 \text{ or } 57$$

Thus, a sample size of 57 would be required for the same level of statistical precision. A sample size of approximately 60 was considered reasonable for the automatic scale case cited above, with a total sample of 9 × 60 or 540.

A few words of caution are appropriate here. First, it does no good to select a basis for stratification which cannot be implemented. Thus if the sample is being drawn from a master population roster, as was done for the case above, the data base already must be categorized according to the basis for stratification chosen. Second, the level of precision required in each cell often varies considerably. If a cell sample size of 30 had been used in the above example instead of 60, with population proportions of .7 and .3 to be estimated at the 90 percent level of confidence, the error in the estimate would have been $\pm$ 13.76 percent instead of $\pm$ 10 percent.[3] In the above example, it is likely that one or more cells were not as critical as others. In such a case it would be more desirable to reallocate the sample (or reduce it) and tolerate the slightly larger estimating errors in the noncritical cells.

Quantitative Questionnaire Design and Interview Procedures

The quantitative phase usually requires only a short pre-structured questionnaire which can normally be administered by telephone, as noted previously in Figure 11.7. In order to understand the logic behind the quantitative questionnaire design and survey procedures, the reader should recall that one of the authors' primary objectives has been to devise a more efficient total process for evaluating and guiding the development of new products. This objective is reached, in part, by selecting and limiting the tasks undertaken at each phase of the research procedure (exploratory, qualitative, and quantitative). The reader will recall that the exploratory phase is designed to obtain a moderate amount of information from a very small (6–10) sample. The qualitative phase requires a large amount of information from a moderate-sized (15–30) sample, and the quantitative phase, which we now address, requires a small amount of information from a relatively large (200–2000) sample.

A logical two-part question is, (1) How can a small amount of information suffice at this important step? and (2) Why is it not possible to obtain the same information at an earlier point in the research process? The answer to both questions is essentially the same. It is only because of the depth of understanding gained during the qualitative phase that enough insight has been obtained to know which of many selected facts are key indicators of requirements. Therefore, it is only *after* gaining this depth of understanding that such a survey and questionnaire *could* be designed. The conduct of the quantitative study is also dependent on the qualitative study to define the segments and to indicate which persons (or positions) within the firms to be surveyed have and are willing to provide the necessary information.

The qualitative survey also indicates the specialized terminology or jargon to use in communicating with such persons and indicates which of several key items of data the respondent will have available and be willing to disclose. For example, a given supermarket manager may not be willing to disclose the actual volume of meat sold, yet he or she might be willing to disclose the total square footage of the store, or the percentage of total space devoted to the meat section, or the total number of employees, and possibly the number of people who work in the meat section; he may even disclose the store's total weekly sales volume. From any one, or, better, from a combination of factors such as these, the dollar volume of the meat department could be estimated with reasonable precision. Thus, one important output of the qualitative phase is this knowledge concerning which of many facts certain persons in the stores know and are willing to disclose. Without this input the quantitative survey either would not be possible at all, or it would not provide the quality of information made possible by the sequential process.

The quantitative questionnaire is usually one to three pages in length and should be prestructured to facilitate obtaining the needed information in ten to fifteen minutes via the telephone. Sometimes separate questionnaires (of approximately the same length) are needed for different market segments surveyed if the terminology and requirements differ markedly among segments. The questionnaire used to obtain information by telephone from building supply outlets regarding cultured marble vanity tops is shown in Figure 11.8. This questionnaire was designed to test two principal hypotheses: (1) there is sufficient market within 500 miles of Holland, Michigan to justify entering the market, and (2) there is a lack of competition in the market.

Because questionnaires such as the one shown can be highly structured, the telephone interviewing can often be contracted to a market research firm with a staff of trained professional interviewers.

Output and Conclusion from Quantitative Phase

The primary outputs from this phase are the measurement of

the market potential for each of the major segments and the measurement of the extent of competitive penetration in each segment. When these outputs are combined with the detailed requirements information from the qualitative phase, intelligent decisions can be made concerning which segments offer the greatest relative profit potential, and what product configurations should be developed in order to compete effectively in each segment. Moreover, a meaningful return on investment (ROI) calculation can be made to evaluate the investment decision.

On the other hand, if the market segments do not offer sufficient potential, or competition has already penetrated to such an extent that entry would be unprofitable, the project may be terminated or shelved, as could have been done following the qualitative phase. In most instances the output of the quantitative phase provides the basis for planning the subsequent technical development program. The firm can proceed confidently with that program because the major cause of new product failure has been eliminated: the failure to analyze the market need in sufficient depth.

Success is not virtually guaranteed at this point, however. Recall from Chapter 1 that there are a host of pitfalls to be avoided. For example, there still can be technical problems, and there are other marketing strategy variables which must receive proper consideration. Recall in Chapter 2, Figure 2.4, that a marketing strategy consists of five elements: the definition of the target market (segments) and the specification of the 4 P's, Product, Price, Promotion, and Place (channels of distribution).

Only the first three of these elements (target market, product, and price) have been addressed directly by the three-phase research program. However, considerable information will have been obtained regarding the nature of promotion needed and appropriate channels of distribution. This information can be used to help design any subsequent market tests or introduction strategy.

Time and Effort for Industrial/Commercial Versus Military/Aerospace Products

Recall from Chapter 1 that our new product procedures had their genesis in work on military electronic countermeasures in the early 1950's. Over the ensuing years, we have helped with the development of many other products for military/aerospace applications. These have included navigation and positioning equipment, artillery and airborne radars, airborne power generation equipment and circuit protection, fuel and lubrication pumps, flight controls and cockpit displays, to mention just a few examples.

A comparison of the time and effort needed to research the product requirement for Industrial/Commercial versus Military/Aerospace products is shown in Table 11-2. There are two major differences in the time and effort required for the two classes of products.

First, the qualitative requirements research stage usually takes about 50 percent longer for military/aerospace products. The reason is twofold: the need must be understood in relation to a complex mission environment, and also all technologies involved are pushing the state of the art. One example is the development of the Data Transfer System by Lear Siegler, Inc. for mission data transfer for the F-4 fighter, which required use of the latest technology to compress memory into a pocket-sized module, shown in Figure 11.9. In a case such as this, it usually takes a little longer to uncover the "true" technical requirements which are both militarily useful and technically feasible and, moreover, permit the product to succeed *and* make a profit.

QUANTITATIVE QUESTIONNAIRE
FOR BUILDING SUPPLY OUTLETS

I represent a manufacturer who feels his company has developed a better way of producing cultured marble vanity tops. We're trying to find out more about the market for them.

1. Do you sell vanity tops?
2. Do you sell cultured marble tops?
   Before going into production we'd like to know if the market for cultured marble vanity tops is worth going after.
3. Are cultured marble tops a large part of your vanity top sales? Half? Smaller?

continued on p. 165

164

a. Are these cultured marble tops catching on or is it a passing fad? Why do you feel this is the situation?

b. Do you think cultured marble will be outmoded by another material for vanity top application? Why? How soon?

4. Are your sales of cultured marble vanity tops increasing? Decreasing?

Along with improving the product physically, our goal is to improve the services to the outlets. We understand that there are both good and poor suppliers of cultured marble and we'd like to know what areas need improving.

a. Is delivery time adequate?

b. Are there any problems with consistent design patterns or color consistency between tops?

Is this important?

5. Who supplies you with cultured marble vanity tops?

6. Are they local? Out-of-state?

a. Have you had any problems with the cultured marble tops after they've been sold? What problems?

b. How long have you been handling these tops?

c. Can they be repaired in the field?

7. Have you had any problems with scratching?

Our manufacturing process will be more efficient than the processes presently used by many cultured marble manufacturers; consequently, we think we would be able to lower the prices of these tops.

a. Could you give me an idea of what retail prices we would have to compete against—say for a standard 3- or 4-foot vanity top with integral bowl?

3-foot _____

4-foot _____

8. Would you be interested in handling a cultured marble vanity top with an integral bowl that could be retailed as low as a typical plastic, e.g., formica, counter top with an inlaid porcelain bowl? (This would be equivalent to about $8 per linear foot for the marble vanity top, including integral bowl.)

9. Could you give me a guess of about how many vanity tops of all types you sell per month or year?

10. About how many of these are marble?

11. About how many cultured marble vanity tops could you sell if they retailed at half the present price?

Thank you.

Note: Presented with cooperation and permission of Donnelly Mirrors, Inc., Holland, Michigan.

Figure 11.8

TABLE 11-2

TIME AND EFFORT: INDUSTRIAL/COMMERCIAL VERSUS MILITARY/AEROSPACE PRODUCTS

Step	Industrial/Commercial		Military/Aerospace	
	Time (wks)	Man-hours	Time (wks)	Man-hours
1. Screen	1	8–12	1	8–12
a. Review & assign priority	1	6–10	1	6–10
2. Exploratory Research	4–8	160–360	4–8	160–360
a. Review	1	10–20	1	10–20
3. Qualitative Research	10–20	500–2000	10–20	750–3000
a. Review	1	20–40	1	20–40
4. Quantitative Research	8–12	320–960	1–3	40–120
a. Review	1	10–20	1	10–20
b. ROI, pro forma	2–3	40–120	2–3	40–120
c. Review	1	8–12	1	8–12
Totals	30–49	1082–3554	23–40	1052–3714
5. Establish R&D program				
6. Build prototype				
7. Pilot production				
8. Finalize production model and marketing mix				
9. Start full-scale production and marketing				

Second, note in Table 11-2 that the Quantitative Research phase is much shorter for military/aerospace products than for industrial/commercial ones. The reason is that the military/aerospace market is so concentrated that after completing the qualitative phase the analyst will probably have talked to almost every key decision maker. Although there may be uncertainty concerning the number of airplanes, tanks, or missiles to be built, which incorporate the proposed system, the uncertainty cannot be reduced much further by additional research. The analyst should already have spoken to the people who have the best insights into further plans.

Of course, additional investigation of international markets, such as NATO countries, may be appropriate. The latest published Department of Defense plans should always be checked,

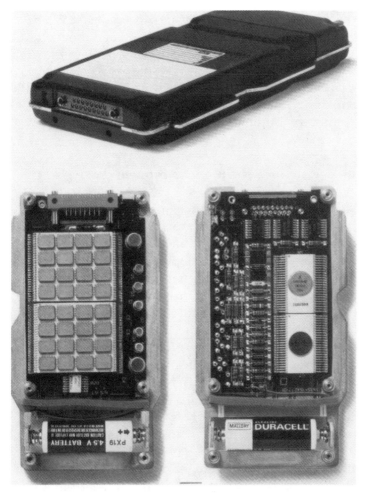

Figure 11.9 Lear Siegler's Data Transfer Module.

and input may be sought from the firm's political analyst in Washington for the latest projections on expenditures.

Note in the figure that the total time and effort for military/ aerospace products is usually a little less than that for industrial/ commercial products. However, this is a broad generalization, subject to major exceptions, especially when the "product" is a major weapons system.

Neither the time nor the manpower estimates shown in the figure would apply to a major system development in either the industrial/commercial or military/aerospace fields. We have seen as much as 18 months and 20,000 to 30,000 man-hours devoted to the requirements analysis for a major commercial computer system. A similar, or greater, effort would be expected for a major military system. The numbers shown in Table 11-2 are thus intended to be typical of a single product for a new or existing aircraft, tank, or other weapons system.

Role of Return on Investment Analysis

Traditional concepts of return on investment (ROI), (payback period, discounted cash flow, net present value, and internal rate of return), can be applied with increasing degrees of precision during the new product development sequence, as indicated earlier in Figure 11.1.[4] A rough estimate can be made at the screening stage, followed by a preliminary estimate at the conclusion of the quantitative research (step 4), and a final, most accurate estimate can be made after the final production model of the product has been designed.

The accuracy of the estimates depends on the quality of information available for analysis. In all techniques for ROI analysis, the two items of information which most affect the accuracy of the ROI estimates, 1) the sales forecast and 2) the manufacturing costs, are also the most difficult to determine early in the new product development process.[5]

Thus, at the screening step only a very rough estimate of sales and manufacturing costs is possible. However, at the end of the quantitative research (step 4), information is available concerning the total requirements for the product as well as market size. Even though the technical development has not begun (with the possible exception of technical feasibility studies), a good base exists for estimating all remaining costs (R&D, production, and marketing), as well as the potential sales. Thus, the precision of the ROI estimate made at this point is much greater than it was at the screening step.

Note, however, that until the quantitative research has been completed, very little confidence can be placed in the ROI analysis. Although some improvement can be made at the conclusion of the exploratory and qualitative phases, an estimate of one of the most important variables in the ROI calculation is still missing until the quantitative step: the sales potential.

For these reasons, we suggest that any ROI calculations made prior to the completion of the quantitative stage be taken "with a huge grain of salt," because of the inherent imprecision. You may ask, but what about ROI estimates made by firms which do not use our procedures? Our answer is simply that until information, such as that produced by the qualitative and quantitative research phases is available, ROI calculations are very little more than "whistling in the dark." The fundamental problem with the use of ROI analysis in connection with new product development decisions lies in not having reliable information on which to base the calculations. The fact that our methods directly address this problem is an important additional reason why our procedures enhance the success of the total product development process.

The Role of Market Tests

At the beginning of this chapter we presented a total outline of the new product development process for industrial/commercial products. At that point we briefly discussed the role of market tests of pilot production units (Figure 11.1, step 7), which follows the engineering test of prototypes (step 6).

It is during the initial market test phase that further information can be obtained to improve the final marketing strategy. The term "market test" is somewhat misleading. Properly used, a "market test" is actually an additional *research phase*, used especially to confirm and adjust the promotion, distribution, and pricing strategy. The research is conducted by means of "tests" of different strategy elements in different market segments.

The importance of market tests of new industrial/commercial products is usually related to the degree of emotive elements inherent (1) in the fundamental need, and (2) in the purchasing process.

As we shall explain further in the next chapter, the research techniques employed in the present chapter are not well suited to evaluate the importance (and thus the price implications) of emotive elements in either case. The techniques are, however, capable of *identifying* those elements. The only conclusive way to evaluate the significance of the emotive elements is to construct one or more market test situations and observe the reactions of the purchasing agents, purchasing committee members, design engineers, etc., and finally the users of the new product. The marketing strategy variables which especially require evaluation are the content, type, and amount of advertising and promotional materials, the type and amount of personal selling effort, and the effect of different price levels and combinations of price level and product/service options.

Unfortunately, rather than taking an experimental approach as is usually done to evaluate the same type of variables with new consumer products, the industrial/commercial new product developer often uses a "single cell" design of experiment. That is, he "guesstimates" the optimum combination, and then starts adjusting the marketing mix when it does not work as expected. There are a number of rationalizations given for this approach, such as shortness of product life cycle, absence of emotive elements, etc. However, it has been our observation that in most cases it has been the lack of understanding of the techniques and benefits derived from a more sophisticated approach that has inhibited their usefulness in industrial/commercial markets. This observation has been reinforced repeatedly during the past few years by executives of firms producing industrial/commercial products who have attended the authors' seminars on Planned Innovation. We have received enthusiastic response to the inclusion of product development techniques for consumer products as part of the seminars for firms producing industrial/commercial products. The significance and role of the techniques for industrial/commercial products will become apparent from our discussion in the following chapter.

Summary

In this chapter we have explained the general sequence of activities needed to properly evaluate and guide the development of new industrial/commercial products. The logic and methods involved in the three-stage research procedure have been explained. These procedures can overcome the major problem in new product development: the lack of in-depth understanding of market needs. The chapter concludes with a discussion of the relationships among the techniques presented and the specification of all marketing strategy variables, and suggests that techniques used in evaluating consumer products have application in defining market strategy variables for industrial/commercial products as well.

Footnotes to Chapter 11

[1]Frank R. Bacon, Jr. and Richard A. Lewis, "Progress in the Development of Quantitative Market Requirements Models for Use in Long-Range Product Planning." Paper presented at the 7th International Meeting of the Institute of Management Sciences, New York, October, 1960.

[2]If the sample size is larger than 10 percent of the population, the finite correction factor $\sqrt{\frac{N-n}{N}}$ should be applied to reduce the standard error of the proportion $\sqrt{\frac{pq}{n}}$, and thus reduce the sample size (N = population size and n = sample size).

[3]$e = z\sqrt{\frac{pq}{n}} = 1.645\sqrt{\frac{(.7)(.3)}{30}} = 13.76\%.$

[4]Philip A. Scheuble, Jr., "ROI for New-Product Planning," *Harvard Business Review* (November-December 1964), pp. 110–20; and Joel S. Greenberg, "Risk Analysis," *Astronautics and Aeronautics* (November 1974), pp. 48–57.

[5]For techniques used in handling risk in investment decisions, see: David B. Hertz, "Risk Analysis in Capital Investment," *Harvard Business Review*, Vol. 42 (January–February 1964), pp. 91–106; David B. Hertz, "Investment Policies That Pay Off," *Harvard Business Review* (January–February 1968), pp. 96–108; and E. Eugene Carter, "What Are the Risks in Risk Analysis?" *Harvard Business Review*, Vol. 50, No. 4 (July–August 1972), pp. 72–82.

Chapter 12

Research Procedures for Consumer Products

In this chapter on procedures for evaluating consumer products, we do not provide the detail on research techniques, as we attempted to do for industrial/commercial products in the last chapter. Rather, the purpose is to show how consumer procedures, largely developed and perfected by others, fit into the overall framework of procedures derived by the authors.[1,2,3] The purpose is also to explain *why* other procedures are required to handle the analysis of need associated with consumer products. An additional purpose of the chapter is to illustrate how the procedures required for industrial/commercial products and those for consumer products can be combined to analyze the requirements for products which jointly serve both types of markets.

Consumer New Product Development Sequence

A generalized sequence of steps for the development of new consumer products is shown in Figure 12.1, including approximate lengths of time required for major phases of activity. The first step, the screening process, is the same as for industrial/commercial products. That is, screening criteria must be drawn up after restatement of objectives and completion of a strength and weakness analysis. The screening criteria are then applied to new product opportunities as is done for industrial/commercial products. From this point on, however, the procedures for consumer products differ markedly from those for industrial/commercial products.

Concept Tests

Note that the next step in the sequence following screening, shown in Figure 12.1, is a concept test. This step is somewhat similar to the exploratory phase discussed in Chapter 11 in that it

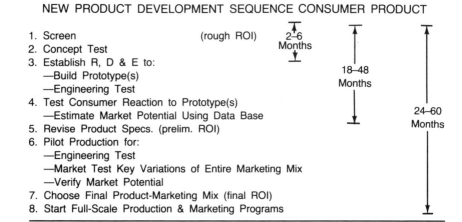

NEW PRODUCT DEVELOPMENT SEQUENCE CONSUMER PRODUCT

1. Screen   (rough ROI)   2–6 Months
2. Concept Test
3. Establish R, D & E to: 18–48 Months
   —Build Prototype(s)
   —Engineering Test
4. Test Consumer Reaction to Prototype(s)
   —Estimate Market Potential Using Data Base   24–60 Months
5. Revise Product Specs. (prelim. ROI)
6. Pilot Production for:
   —Engineering Test
   —Market Test Key Variations of Entire Marketing Mix
   —Verify Market Potential
7. Choose Final Product-Marketing Mix (final ROI)
8. Start Full-Scale Production & Marketing Programs

Figure 12.1

is a preliminary evaluation of the product-market concept. The concept test, however, focuses only on whether the idea for the new product makes sense to the potential users. Other aspects of the requirements for successful innovation included in the exploratory stage of the industrial/commercial procedure—the technical, production, marketing, and competitive aspects—usually cannot be given explicit attention at this point because the product-market is not defined well enough to do so. However, as soon as the product-market definition is clarified, we recommend that these issues be addressed, as we demonstrate with the "Handi-Voice[R]" example later in the chapter.

A concept test can take many forms. Some firms use a one- or two-sentence description on a 3" × 5" card. In such cases a group of consumers known to be in the intended target market are assembled (usually by a market research firm) and given a stack of cards to evaluate. They are often asked to place the concepts in three categories such as (1) definitely would *not* be interested in purchasing, (2) undecided, and (3) definitely *would* be interested in purchasing.

A technique used in the package food industry is to prepare a picture of the box which might contain the new product together with a picture and text on the box describing the product.

A technique used in fashion- or style-conscious industries such as clothing or automotive design is to build life-size prototypes and let a carefully chosen sample of people in the intended target market view them and give their reaction. The initial concept-testing activity may take two to six months, as shown in Figure 12.1, before starting development of a prototype.

Requirements for Successful Concept Testing

Regardless of which technique is used, there are two primary requirements for a successful concept test. First, the concept must be accurately communicated to the respondents and understood by them. Among the techniques described above, the one-sentence description technique runs a large risk of being misunderstood or misinterpreted. The picture and description on a box of food runs less risk, and the actual prototype of clothing or an automobile runs the lowest risk.

As can be seen, the risk of misinterpretation involved is usually inversely proportional to the amount of investment in the mechanism for communicating the concept. Many firms say the only safe procedure is to build an exact replica or prototype for initial evaluation. If the cost of the prototype is small, there is no question of the desirability. However, a new food product may require many thousands of dollars before a "prototype" can be available to test. The best choice is always a tradeoff between risk and cost.

The second aspect of concept testing which is absolutely necessary for success is that the persons reacting to the concept test be members of the intended target market. The opinions of persons outside the target market are next to worthless. This further underscores the importance of a marketing orientation for success in new product development. Remember, a marketing strategy consists first of the definition of the target market, followed by the specification of the product, price, promotion, and price variables.

Prototypes Are Used to Determine
Actual Product Requirements

Following the successful completion of the concept test, the third step shown in Figure 12.1 is the establishment of a technical development program (Research, Development, and Engineering) in order to develop prototypes of the new product. There are two purposes for the prototypes: (1) for engineering (technical) evaluation, and (2) for consumer evaluation (Step 4 in the figure).

The sequence of steps 3, 4, and 5 roughly parallels the qualitative phase for industrial/commercial products. Recall that the general purpose of the qualitative phase is to determine the range of variation in product requirements. The same is generally true for these steps in the consumer new-product development sequence: the purpose is to determine the product requirements. What appears to be a contradiction—that we develop a product to tell us what to develop—is exactly what is done. But it is not a contradiction. It is simply the technique necessary to define the requirements for consumer products where the emotive elements of need often dominate the demand determinants.

In such cases, the only way a consumer *can* give accurate information concerning the new product requirements is with reference to a close facsimile of the actual product. Ideally, this facsimile can be used exactly as the final product would be used, as for example, a cake mix, or a new home appliance. Only then can the consumer accurately tell what he or she likes or does not like about the new product, because only then can all the significant product attributes be evaluated relative to the environment of the total elements of need, both emotive and economic.

Returning to Step 4 in Figure 12.1, note that after the consumer reaction to the prototype, one can make an estimate of market potential. This is possible with consumer products if most of the consumer subjects chosen were in fact in the target market, and if a suitable consumer data base has been maintained by the firm. Large firms in consumer product fields would normally be expected to comply with both conditions. Small firms also can comply by working with professional market research firms that can properly choose the subjects, conduct the tests, and provide a suitable consumer data base which can be used to make quantitative estimates for their clients.

Several Iterations May By Necessary

After completing the consumer evaluation of the product prototype, it can be anticipated that revisions will be needed, as shown in Step 5 in Figure 12.1. However, what is not shown is that Steps 3, 4, and 5 may be repeated several times before a suitable product is developed. It is difficult to generalize about how long it will take to perform these steps, but we have observed that the minimum time from project start to completion of step 5 is about

18 months, and may be as great as 48 months, as is indicated in Figure 12.1. And when the final design is completed, a preliminary return on investment (ROI) analysis can be made based on the consumer reaction together with a suitable data base, as described above. This is also indicated in the figure at Step 5.

Determining the Remaining Marketing Mix

Let us presume that a suitable product design has evolved from the previous steps. In Step 6 we tackle the remaining market strategy variables: price, promotion, and place channels. Of course, final engineering tests are conducted on the product design, and a suitable pilot production run must be made in order to conduct the necessary market tests to evaluate the price, promotion, and place variables just mentioned above. The result of the test will provide additional validation of market potential, as is also shown in the figure. In this way the step provides the same output as the quantitative phase for industrial/commercial products. However, Step 6 in the consumer sequence also provides additional information concerning the remaining market strategy variables not obtained until later (Step 7) in the industrial/commercial sequence shown earlier in Figure 11.1. The market test also provides a final estimate of market protential with the effect of all marketing mix variables in operation to affect sales.

The reason that the price, promotion, and place variables must be given explicit attention in the consumer new product development process relates back to the determinants of need. For consumer products, emotive elements always play a significant role in demand. The emotive factors must be addressed in all elements of the marketing mix. For example, the price it is possible to obtain is related to both the place(s) where the product can be obtained, and to the type and level of advertising employed. Thus, the interaction of these three important variables must be evaluated, together with the product variable itself.

Market testing constitutes a major aspect of the new product development activity—and must also be reflected in the budget— for many consumer products such as cosmetics, nonprescription drugs, packaged foods, etc. The only way the level and interaction of all the marketing mix variables can be assessed is in the actual market environment. Despite the many problems inherent in the procedures employed (such as conscious efforts by competitors to distort test results), this has been a fruitful area for the application of experimental design techniques and appropriate statistical methods for analysis.[4]

It is only after the effect of these important marketing variables has been determined that the final product-marketing mix can be chosen (Step 7, Figure 12.1) and the full-scale production and marketing programs launched (Step 8). Of course, it is possible to make a "guesstimate" of the optimum mix of these variables and proceed with the market introduction. This is often done with industrial/commercial products and for consumer products which are intended for familiar target markets using well-established marketing procedures where the variables are not so critical. Even though the product-marketing mix can be adjusted once experience is gained, the risk of failure is increased without market testing; furthermore, potential profits may be foregone if substantial adjustments are necessary. Nevertheless, many firms without resources or marketing sophistication must rely on minimal procedures. Those whose "guesstimates" are correct survive and those whose are grossly in error often join the ranks of business failures.

Examples of Consumer Product Developments

To illustrate the similarity, and to show the diversity in procedures and levels of effort needed for the development of consumer products, we have chosen two examples. First, is the development of the "Quick Shift™" bicycle shifting mechanism by AMF, shown in Figure 12.2, and second is the development of the solid dietary food bar "Figurines[R]" by Pillsbury, shown in Figure 12.3. Both represented new products for more or less familiar markets using existing channels of distribution.

The "Quick Shift™" Development[5]

The sequence of steps involved in the "Quick Shift™" development is summarized in Figure 12.4. Shown is the time from the start of the project to the start and finish of each step. For proprietary reasons the manpower effort cannot be shown. It can be said, however, that the total effort required was quite modest.

178

Figure 12.2 AMF's Quick Shift^{TM}

Returning to the figure, note that the project began with focus group interviews of bicycle owners to explore "what is wrong with present bicycles." Group interviews were held with owners of 1-speed, 3-speed, 5-speed, and 10-speed bicycles. From these interviews it was confirmed that problems with the shifting of 10-speed derailleur models was the major concern to most owners who used the bicycle mainly for recreational purposes (not professional racers). There was a strongly felt need for a simple-to-operate gear shift mechanism which clearly indicated the gear chosen. A functional specification of the desired mechanism was defined, and then discussed with the division engineering design staff.

Figure 12.3   Pillsbury's Figurines[R]

The engineering staff launched an internal and external search of all known technical approaches to the functional requirement (Step 2 in the figure). Based on these analyses a technical approach was chosen which, it was believed, would meet the requirements, and provide patent protection as well.

180

"QUICK SHIFT"™ DEVELOPMENT		Time from Start of Project (Months)
1. Focus-Group Studies of improvements needed in bicycles; select gear shift	Start	0
	Finish	3
2. Engineering evaluation of possible technical approaches	Start	3
	Finish	4
3. Engineering development; build prototype of most promising design approach; apply for patent	Start	4
	Finish	28
4. Show prototype to buyers for major retail chains (after obtaining patent); estimate market potential	Start	28
	Finish	30
5. Obtain consumer reaction to prototype in a central location test	Start	30
	Finish	34
6. Obtain estimates for tooling costs	Start	34
	Finish	37
7. Make engineering production model	Start	37
	Finish	39
8. Tool for production	Start	39
	Finish	42
9. Start production to build inventory for introduction	Start	42
	Finish	45
10. Release to selected retail chains, start national advertising	Start	48

Figure 12.4

The engineering development (Step 3) which required 24 months, resulted in a prototype and a patent. As soon as patent protection was assured, the prototype was shown to the buyers at well-known retail chains who already handled the top-of-the-line AMF bicycles for their evaluation (Step 4). Their estimates of market potential were based on existing sales of bicycles by the retail chains. It was decided that these channels would reach a large portion of the intended target market.

Upon receiving a strong positive response from the major buyers, a test of consumer reaction to the product was performed, using a central location test in a medium-sized midwestern city (Step 5). Two hundred owners of ten-speed bicycles were shown prototype bicycles containing several new product improvements, including the Quick Shift™. Attitudes toward each new product improvement were obtained, including the additional amount of money they would pay for the Quick Shift™ in comparison with the price of a standard derailleur. This was, in effect, a concept test using prototypes of the actual product to represent the concept. Based on strong confirmation received from the consumer concept test, together with that already received from major buyers, the decision was made to proceed with the project.

Estimates of tooling costs were obtained (Step 6); a production model was finalized (Step 7); tooling for production was obtained (Step 8); and production was begun to build inventory (Step 9) prior to market introduction (Step 10). Since the product was to be initially released through selected major retail distributors, the bulk of the marketing task would be transferred to the channel members, with the exception of supporting national advertising. The entire project, from start to market introduction took 48 months as shown in the figure.

You may logically ask why there was no formal test marketing. There are several reasons. First, the total cost for tooling and for manufacturing the initial inventory prior to market introduction was quite modest—on the order of $100,000. These costs would have been the same if a market test had been done instead.

Second, among the remaining marketing mix variables (i.e., other than product), price, promotion, and place, there was very little uncertainty and therefore little risk. The new product represented at most a logical extension of the existing product, or perhaps only a modification of the existing product. The product was designed for a familiar target market using familiar channels. Thus, well-understood promotional techniques could also be used.

The greatest uncertainty involved price. But here again, the firm had the advice of experienced buyers and merchandising managers of national retail organizations, which sell bicycles to the intended target market. And most importantly, price is the easiest variable to adjust, if necessary, once the product is introduced.

This is especially true if a skimming pricing policy is used (starting high and reducing if necessary).

Finally, by introducing the product through selective distribution, the early phases could represent a sort of "test" marketing effort, if monitored closely. For example, we recommend that a specially designed warranty card be used to obtain rapid feedback from early adopters. Thus adjustments in promotion and price could be made before expanding the distribution.

In summary, a formal test-marketing effort was not chosen because there was too little uncertainty about the marketing mix variables to justify the time and effort. And more precise estimates of sales potential were not believed necessary to justify proceeding. It was believed that the small amount of uncertainty could be resolved by closely monitoring the early results from the selective distribution strategy. In the "Figurines[R]" example below, we describe procedures required when the uncertainty (and risk) is much greater.

Development of Figurines[R6]

At the time the concept for Figurines[R] originated, liquid dietary foods such as "Metrical", "Sego," and "Slender" were gaining in popularity. The idea behind Figurines[R] (Figure 12.3) was that a solid dietary food might be more convenient because it could be stored, carried, and handled more conveniently. For example, women, who were the main consumers of dietary products, might be able to carry the product in their purse, whereas it would be inconvenient to do so with a liquid dietary product. The steps involved in evaluating and developing the concept into the product are shown in Figure 12.5 together with the times for starting and completing each phase.

Focus Group Interviews

To explore the idea that a solid dietary food might be accepted, or even preferred, three focus-group interviews were held with weight-conscious women in middle and upper-middle income brackets (Figure 12.5, step 1), the approximate intended target market. Two of the groups used liquid dietary products and

DEVELOPMENT OF "FIGURINES^R"

	Time from Start of Project (Months)

1. Focus-Group interviews with users and non-users of diet foods	Start	0
	Finish	1
2. Concept test for solid dietary food—using full-color print ads on posterboards—Re: Proposed-vs-competing (liquid) dietary foods	Start	4
	Finish	5
3. Begin prototype development	Start	5
	Finish	8
4. Main office taste test of prototype	Start	9
	Finish	10
5. Consumer central location taste tests of improved prototype	Start	10
	Finish	11
6. Initiate pilot plant production	Start	11
	Finish	13
7. Consumer central location test to choose name for product (using full-color print ads on posterboards)	Start	12
	Finish	13
8. Consumer central location taste test of product from pilot plant	Start	13
	Finish	14
9. Consumer in-home use test (with product from pilot plant)	Start	14
	Finish	15
10. Results from independent testing lab reveal insufficient protein content	Start	14
	Finish	15
11. Learned that oven manufacturer will be unable to deliver required equipment on schedule		15
12. Reformulate product to increase protein	Start	15
	Finish	16
13. Repeat steps 4, 5, 6, 8, and 9 with reformulated product	Start	16
	Finish	23
14. Reformulate product to improve flavor (with increased calorie content)	Start	23
	Finish	24
15. Repeat steps 5, 6, 8, and 9 (again)	Start	24
	Finish	26

continued on p. 185

16. Main office taste tests to determine effect of remaining on shelf for X days (shelf life)	Start	32
	Finish	33
17. Start pilot production for market test		33
18. Consumer central location test to evaluate alternative TV commercials	Start	36
	Finish	36
19. Conduct test marketing in four cities to evaluate price, shelf location, and level of advertising	Start	36
	Finish	47
20. Begin national market introduction		48

Note: Presented with cooperation and permission of Pillsbury, Inc., Minneapolis, Minnesota.

Figure 12.5

one did not. Artists' drawings of seven new product concepts were used to stimulate discussion about likes and dislikes of liquid dietary products and attitudes toward possible solid dietary foods of various types. The concept of a solid food "stick" or "cookie" with controlled calories received strong support.

Concept Test

Fueled with encouragement, the firm planned a concept test with a larger group of women with the same characteristics as those in the focus-group interviews (step 2 in Figure 12.5). A sample of over 800 women was selected by a market research firm, half of whom were users of liquid dietary products and half of whom were not. Eight product concepts were illustrated on full-color posterboards representing an advertisement for the product concepts. Results of the concept test indicated that current users of liquid dietary products would be a primary target market for one or two of the solid dietary food concepts tested.

Prototype Development and Taste Test Within Firm

The development of a prototype solid dietary bar took about three months (Step 3 in the figure). A taste test was immediately initiated (Step 4), using 60 female employees to sample six products over a two-month period. After several tests (with the product reformulated after each one), a suitable product was devised and formulated in several flavors.

Consumer Taste Test

A consumer central location test was again performed, this time with 128 women in the target market, to compare the different flavors with those of competing products (Step 5 in the figure). This test showed two flavors (sweet and fruit) superior to competing products.

Pilot plant production of these flavors was then begun in order to manufacture product for the later in-home use test.

Selection of Product Name

At the same time, it was necessary to decide on a name for the product for use in subsequent in-home consumer testing. A central location test was devised (Step 7) for this purpose. Posterboards containing 8 different full color advertisements of the solid dietary food product with different names were presented to 150 general shopers. The name "Figurines[R]" emerged as the best for the product concept.

Taste Test of Pilot Production

As soon as the product became available from the pilot plant (Step 8), it was taste-tested to be certain it was suitable for the in-home use test. The taste test was performed at a central location in a shopping center with 48 women in the target market. The product produced by the pilot plant was compared with competing products and found to be strongly preferred.

Extended In-Home Use Test

Confident of the product quality and taste, researchers devised an in-home use test to evaluate the product over an extended period of usage (Step 9). A market research firm conducted the test in ten cities with a total of about 800 consumers. Current users of liquid dietary products or serious dieters were identified through door-to-door sampling in medium- to high-income neighborhoods. Consumers falling in the target market were given samples of the product to try over a 3- to 4-week period, after which they reported their evaluation by questionnaire.

Murphy's Law at Work

With positive results from the consumer in-home use test, the product design was considered complete, and plans were begun for the market test to evaluate the remaining marketing mix variables—price, promotion, and place. However, at this point two problems arose (Steps 10 and 11). First, analysis by an independent laboratory of the protein content of the bar turned out to be less than had been specified as desirable, and second, the manufacturer of the special ovens required to produce the product informed Pillsbury that the ovens could not be delivered on schedule; Murphy's law strikes again! Actually the delay in equipment delivery was not critical because much additional work was required on the product.

Redesign of Product

Given the laboratory results, there was nothing to do but reformulate the product to increase its protein content (Step 12). Although this was done within about one month, it was then necessary to repeat the sequence of consumer tests to be certain that the reformulated product would be acceptable (Step 13). Repeating these tests required six to seven months as indicated in the figure.

Unfortunately, the results of the second in-home use test (with the reformulated product) indicated that the redesigned product did not have an adequate level of consumer acceptance. It was determined that the reformulated product did not have enough flavor. The deficiency did not show up in the one-exposure central location tests, and became apparent only after extended use. Back to the drawing board again!

Second Product Redesign

Resolving the problem of inadequate flavor was not as simple as increasing the protein. It is easy enough to increase the flavor, but what increases flavor? You guessed it, *calories*! Thus, a compromise had to be struck between increase in flavor and increase in calories. The net result was an increase in calories (Step 14). The question now arose, will the calorie-conscious target market accept the product with increased calories even though it has improved flavor? The answer lay in repeating (for a second time) the consumer testing (Step 15). Fortunately all signals were "go" at the conclusion of the series of tests this time. After it was determined that the product would have adequate shelf life (Step 16), the product design was finally complete.

Market Test

Market testing is needed whenever there is considerable uncertainty about the elements of the marketing mix because the choice can greatly affect the sales realized. In this case there was uncertainty about the optimum price, level of advertising, and where the product should be positioned (shelf location) within supermarkets. There was no doubt that supermarkets were the correct overall channel to reach the target market.

To prepare for the market test, it was necessary to begin pilot production to build an inventory of product to use in the test (Step 17). It was also necessary to make a final choice between two television commercials. This was done with the aid of a consumer central location test (Step 18).

An experimental design was used in the market test (Step 19). The design included a combination of four cities, two price levels, two levels of advertising, and two shelf locations—with breakfast foods and with dietary foods. The test was run for about 10 months to allow usage patterns to stabilize and for production ovens to be installed. It may seem that the test was run longer than necessary, but there was a strong desire to be absolutely sure of the product, because of the many reversals experienced during development and to have production volumes developed before introducing the product nationally.

After analyzing results from the test marketing, the optimum combination of price level, level of advertising, and shelf location was chosen, and a final estimate of national sales was made. Introduction of the product to the national market was done in phases. First, coverage was expanded throughout the region of the test market. Then other major regions were entered one after the other, over a period of several months.

Time and Costs

At the time of its development, the concept of a solid dietary food was a new product for Pillsbury as well as for the market. The particular target market (users of liquid dietary foods and serious dieters) was also new for Pillsbury, although they were familiar with the channels and promotional techniques. There was much to learn and many problems to overcome. Had the technical problem (insufficient protein content) not surfaced unexpectedly at the end of the first in-home use test, and had the oven supplier been able to supply production equipment on time, this development probably would have been completed in 24 to 30 months instead of 48.

In many respects, however, this case is typical of the many unforeseen problems which can arise in any new product effort. The case is also typical of the sophistication and dedication necessary for getting the product right before releasing it, which is characteristic of large packaged food companies such as Pillsbury.

In the above description, we have included the number of persons and cities involved in the various product and market tests so that you can see the magnitude of the evolving effort involved. In 1980 dollars the cost of each focus-group interview and related concept tests will range from $2,000 to $5,000. Central location tests will range from $5,000 to $7,000, and the in-home use tests will cost $100,000 to $150,000. A market test of the type described will cost $150,000 to $250,000 exclusive of product sold. Had the Figurines[R] development gone smoothly, the series of consumer tests to develop the product would have cost about $200,000 in 1980 dollars, and a like amount for the market test. However, because of the problems encountered, much more than this was needed. It should also be noted that this figure does not include costs of technical development, prototype production, or the special equipment required for production.

Why Was It Worth It?

In comparison to the Quick Shift[TM] development, Figurines[R] took about the same amount of time, but cost many times more. How could its development be justified? Easily: look at the relative sizes of the two markets involved and lengths of product life cycles anticipated. Note especially that Figurines[R] takes advantage of three fundamental long-run trends (as shown earlier in Figure 4.4): (1) The trend toward health- and weight-consciousness, (2) the changing role of women in society and work role, and (3) the rising income levels, especially of middle and upper-middle income groups. Thus, an increasing market with a long product life cycle can be anticipated. A twenty-year life may not be unreasonable. Think how long other major package foods have been on the market: Betty Crocker cake mixes, Bisquick, Wheaties, Corn Flakes, etc.

Finally, let us conclude this case example with the most important reason that this development should succeed. From the very beginning, Pillsbury defined its target market very specifically and sought to understand an unmet need; after the need had been defined they did not release the product until it met the need in every respect, even though they had to overcome considerable adversity to do so.

A Comparison: Consumer Versus Industrial/ Commercial Research Procedures

A side-by-side comparison of the procedures for the two types of market environments is presented in Figure 12.6. The screening process (Step 1) is the same in both cases, as was mentioned earlier. The consumer concept test compares roughly with the industrial exploratory stage, although the exploratory research is more comprehensive.

Note that expenditures on research, development, and engineering must be made much earlier in the consumer sequence (and without the benefit of a well-founded ROI analysis) than in the industrial one because it is necessary to build prototypes to obtain consumer reaction in order to further define the product requirements. Therefore, if considerable expense is involved in developing and building the prototypes, the financial risk involved may be considerable, because only the results of the concept test are available to guide the initial development effort. In contrast, to assure that the technical development funds are wisely spent, the industrial sequence has the output from all three phases available for guidance, with excellent input available for the preliminary ROI analysis *before* major expenditures on R&D.

NEW PRODUCT DEVELOPMENT SEQUENCE
INDUSTRIAL VS. CONSUMER

INDUSTRIAL	CONSUMER
1. Screen (Rough ROI)	1. Screen (Rough ROI)
2. Exploratory Research	2. Concept Test
3. Qualitative Research	3. R,D&E
	—Build prototype(s)
	—Engineering test
4. Quantitative Research	4. Consumer Test of Prototype(s)
—Estimate market potential	—Estimate market potential
(Prelim. ROI)	(Prelim. ROI)
5. Establish R&D	5. Revise Product Characteristics
6. Build Prototype	6. Pilot Production of Revised Product
—Engineering test	—Engineering test
	—Market test key variations of entire marketing mix
	—Verify market potential
7. Pilot Production of Prototype	7. Finalize Product-Marketing Mix (Final ROI)
—Test in market environment	
—Verify market potential	
8. Finalize Production Model and Marketing Mix (Final ROI)	8. Start Full-Scale Production and Marketing Program
9. Start Full-Scale Production and Marketing Program	

Figure 12.6

Because of the large emotive elements of need inherent in consumer products, all four marketing variables—product, price, promotion, and place—usually must be researched by means of interaction with consumers as was illustrated in the Figurines[R] example above. This involves Steps 3, 4, 5, and 6 of the consumer sequence. On the other hand, because of the larger economic element of need involved in industrial/commercial products, the product and price variables can be fairly accurately determined with the three-stage research process. The remaining variables, promotion and place, even though less critical for industrial/commercial than consumer products, still must be evaluated in an

191

interactive (market test) mode (Step 7). Of course, the product and price variables can also be examined for final "fine tuning" during the same market tests.

Then in both cases, once all elements of the market strategy have been defined, the full-scale production and market introduction programs can be launched. With this comparison of the two approaches in mind, let us now turn to the situation found quite often where an industrial (or consumer) product must be designed to meet needs characteristic of both consumer and industrial products.

Research Procedures for Joint Consumer-Industrial Product: The HandiVoice[R] Development[7]

The type of situation which requires a mix of research techniques is one where large components of both economic and emotive elements of need exist for an industrial/commercial product. The users may be a firm or institution and/or individuals. This situation often exists in developing medical equipment, such as wheelchairs, kidney dialysis machines, etc. The buyer may be an institution, a doctor, or an individual who purchases the equipment for his or her own personal use. Strong elements of both economic and emotive need are present.

To show how the product requirements would be determined in such a situation, let us consider the recent development of an item of equipment called "HandiVoice[R]" (shown in Figure 12.7). Using a proprietary electronic voice-synthesis technology, this instrument was developed to provide a synthetic voice (speaking ability) for people who were physically unable to speak.[8]

The target market included victims of disabling diseases such as stroke, cerebral palsy, and multiple sclerosis as well as accident victims and individuals having had oral surgery, such as a glossectomized laryngectomy. As can be seen, it was possible to define the target market very precisely. The initial task was to define the product requirements to meet the market need.

Because the individual disabled person would use the instrument as a personal prosthesis, the product had many consumer considerations. On the other hand, such equipment is rarely purchased without a recommendation from a physician, speech

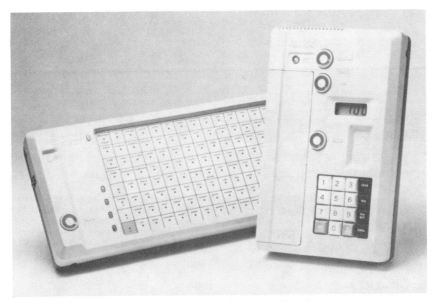

Figure 12.7 Votrax' HandiVoice[R]

pathologist, or similar professional, and money for its purchase frequently comes from institutional sources such as the Veterans Administration or insurance companies. Consequently, this instrument also had many of the characteristics of an industrial/commercial product.

The sequence of steps followed in developing the product is shown in Figure 12.8. Also shown is the total time from start of the project to completion of each activity (the total project took only 22 months), and the man-hours in which new product development personnel were involved in the project. We shall discuss the time and effort after reviewing the steps in the process.

Exploratory Research/Concept Test

After successfully passing the screening (Step 1), a combination industrial/commercial exploratory investigation and consumer concept test was conducted (Step 2). Visits were made to institutions such as special education centers and veterans' hospitals where both professionals and disabled people were located.

193

HANDIVOICE[R] DEVELOPMENT SEQUENCE

		Project Time From Start (Months)	New Product Evaluation and Coordination (Man-hours)
1. Screen		0	10
2. Exploratory research and concept test using flip-charts	Start	¼	400
	Finish	2	
3. Develop two engineering models	Start	1	
	Finish	3,5	
4. Test consumer reaction to first engineering model	Start	3	1400
	Finish	6	
5. Conduct user tests with second tabletop (insti-tutional) model	Start	5	600
	Finish	17	
6. R&D, to develop portable model (the final model)	Start	7	
	Completed	20	600*
7. Market test, portable model	Start	21	
	Finish	22	
8. Full-scale production and distribution	Start	22	
Total		22	3010

*Coordination effort on steps 6, 7, and 8.
Note: Presented with the cooperation and permission of Votrax Division, Federal Screw Works, Troy, Michigan.

Figure 12.8

Hypotheses were generated and tested concerning the market need, the matching of resources, and the existence of a competitive opening. The hypotheses were tested by talking to teachers, speech pathologists, occupational therapists, and similar professionals in education, medicine, and rehabilitation. The traditional four questions were explored: How do these people communicate now? What do existing methods cost now? What is wrong with existing methods? What value would improvements have? Other important exploratory hypotheses were used to explore possible third-party financing for the purchase of such instruments. Because a selling price of several thousand dollars was anticipated, it was important to ascertain that institutional sources of funds such as Blue Cross insurance, Veterans Administration, and Vocational Rehabilitation services would be available to help finance the purchases.

The initial concept test (Step 2) relied upon sketches of conceptual models presented on a flip-chart accompanied by a verbal description of features, operating characteristics, and disabilities served. The professionals and disabled people at the institutions visited were asked to respond to the proposed keyboards, displays, and other features of the conceptual models.

The results of the exploratory investigation indicated a strong need for such a device, with institutional support available to help finance the purchases. The exploratory phase also disclosed that existing methods were so crude and relatively inexpensive (such as pointer boards with symbols or words), that there was little economic basis from which the value of the new equipment could be inferred. The question, "What is it worth for a person to be able to speak?" was answered with emotional responses such as "everything," "the person's whole future," and "more important than mobility (their wheelchair)." It was learned that the negative psychological impact of the inability to communicate was enormous, but the value was obviously derived primarily from the emotive elements of the need.

The response to the concept test was enthusiastic. Typical comments were, "Don't change anything, the device you described is exactly what we need, down to the last detail." Therefore, based on these reactions to the different conceptual models, two configurations were selected for development into working engineering models (Step 3).

Customer Reaction to Engineering Models

After development, which took three months, the first engineering model was shown to the same people who had earlier endorsed the flip-chart concepts (Step 4). Somewhat to the astonishment of the firm, the response to many of the model features

195

was quite negative. The adverse comments included: "That's not what we had in mind"; "the keys are too small"; "the display is hard to see"; etc. Recall our discussion earlier in the chapter concerning the first criterion for concept testing, that the concept must communicate accurately. The flip-chart presentation obviously did not communicate as effectively as the engineering model. However, valuable guidance was obtained from both the flip-chart and the working model.

To insure valid evaluation, a second model (developed in five months) was designed in a tabletop configuration and made available for further user tests. This was called the "institutional" model.

Determining Requirements for the Institutional Model

In designing the institutional model, a key issue to be resolved was the number of words needed in the prestored vocabulary of the speech prosthesis. When asked for the number of words needed, professionals serving nonverbal people responded that 20 words would be entirely adequate. Yet Votrax research staff members had concluded that 400 to 800 words would be needed. Their conclusion had been reached on the basis of word lists devised by language experts interested in finding the minimum number of words needed to communicate effectively in English.

Further exploration revealed that the speech pathologists questioned were responding in terms of the wrong frame of reference, i.e., what could be done with existing techniques, rather than what would be needed for normal comunications. The issue was resolved by giving the speech professionals a list of 400 words selected by the research staff and asking them to cross off those that were *not* needed. Of course, in this frame of reference, the list was *not large* enough. Again, a prototype list of words was needed for the user to *respond to* in order to obtain useful information.

The investigation continued with a series of interactive responses, and limited field tests of the institutional model. This investigation showed conclusively that a key feature for a successful speech prosthesis instrument was portability. The voice synthesis technology embodied in the institutional model was not portable; therefore a major R&D task was defined by the market investigation (Step 6).

Development of Portable Model

The development of a portable, hand-held battery-operated unit was originally conceived as a two-year R&D project; six months into the project, however, a technical breakthrough occurred which greatly accelerated the project's completion. The final, portable model was completed in 13 months, as shown in Step 6 of Figure 12.8. (The development began seven months after the project began and was completed 20 months after the start of the entire project.) After a successful, but limited, field (market) test, similar to that often used for industrial/commercial products (Step 7), full-scale production and marketing was immediately launched using a major hospital supply firm as the channel of distribution (Step 8).

Although there were a number of other emotive issues involved and successfully resolved in the development of this product, such as voice quality, male versus female voice, etc., the issues discussed illustrate the techniques needed for their resolution. Since almost all issues had no economic basis for direct analysis, the iterative response mode was more appropriate, even though this product was designed primarily for purchase by an industrial/commercial target market.

Time and Effort Required

After screening, which took about one week and 10 man-hours of time on the part of personnel responsible for new product development and evaluation (Step 1, Figure 12.8), the combined exploratory research/concept testing phase was started (Step 2). This step required about 2 months' time and 400 man-hours of effort from new products personnel, as shown in the figure. Each of the two engineering prototypes required two months to be built, so that one was available in three months and the other in five months, as shown in Step 3. Using the first model constructed, the concept test with customers required about three months and 1400 man-hours (Step 4).

The second model, the tabletop institutional model, was shown to customers and left with them to use. Conducting these tests and obtaining feedback from those using the device took about 600 man-hours of effort over a 12-month period (Step 5). This led to the requirement for a portable model.

Coordination of effort during the development of the portable model, the short market test, and the introduction through an established hospital supply firm took about 600 man-hours over a 5- or 6-month period as shown in Steps 6, 7, and 8 of Figure 12.8. The total time required for the project and the man-hours for evaluation and coordination by new product personnel were thus 22 months and 3010 man-hours, respectively. As we indicated earlier, the time was unusually short due to the minimal engineering required. The man-hours of evaluation and coordination is typical of industrial/commercial developments, but is much less than normally required for consumer products.

Summary

In this chapter we have described the type of research procedures necessary for consumer products, and have presented examples of activities and time required for typical products. We have explained that it is the emotive elements of need inherent in consumer products which necessitate the difference in research technique for industrial/commercial versus consumer products. The similarities and differences between the research procedures required have been explained.

Products requiring a mix of techniques from both consumer and industrial/commercial approaches have been discussed, and an example illustrating the blend of techniques has been presented. Having thus completed the discussion of techniques for evaluating and guiding the development of new products, we now turn in the next chapter to the important organization and staffing issues associated with the new product function.

Footnotes to Chapter 12

[1]David W. Cravens, Gerald F. Hills, and Robert B. Woodruff, *Marketing Decision Making: Concepts and Strategy*, (Homewood, IL: Richard D. Irwin, Inc., 1976) pp. 488–519.

[2]Robert D. Hisrich and Michael P. Peters, *Marketing a New Product: Its Planning, Development and Control*, (Menlo Park, CA, The Benjamin/ Cummings Publishing Co., Inc., 1978) pp. 108–218.

[3] E. Jerome McCarthy, *Basic Marketing: A Managerial Approach,* 6th Edition (Homewood, IL: Richard D. Irwin, Inc., 1978) pp. 145–257.

[4] David W. Cravens, et al., *Marketing Decision Making.*

[5] Presented with the cooperation and permission of AMF, Inc., White Plains, NY.

[6] Presented with the cooperation and permission of Pillsbury, Inc., Minneapolis, MN.

[7] Presented with the cooperation and permission of Votrax Division of Federal Screw Works, Troy, MI. R. Trezevant Wigfall provided consulting assistance throughout the development and assisted in preparing this case example.

[8] See "Artificial Speech for the Voiceless," *Business Week,* November 28, 1977, p. 46L.

Chapter 13

Organizing and Staffing

In the chapters to this point we have discussed the philosophy of the Bacon/Butler approach and described the research procedures necessary to implement the approach. There are, however, a number of additional factors which directly affect the success of the new product development function. These include the organization and staffing of the function, especially its position within the firm, and the communication and review procedures used. In this chapter we present an expanded treatment of our views on these topics (already presented briefly in Chapter 2), based on our experiences with many firms over the past two decades.

General Organizational and Procedural Requirements

During the past decade or so there has been a good deal written about the issues involved in organizing for new product development.[1,2,3,4] The major questions concern the organizational structure, where the function should be located within the firm, and to whom it should report. Other issues involve the type and size of staff, and communications review procedures required. A complete discussion of these issues would require another book, rather than a single chapter. Since an excellent monograph is available from the Conference Board,[5] we shall limit our discussion to major issues which impinge directly on the success of the procedures presented earlier. We begin our discussion with general criteria for organization and communication and proceed to more specific recommendations concerning organizational forms, staffing, and personnel qualifications.

In Figure 13.1 we show five general organizational and procedural requirements we believe are necessary for success in new product development. They relate directly to the new product

GENERAL ORGANIZATIONAL AND
PROCEDURAL REQUIREMENTS

1. Program must have full support of CEO and/or COO.

2. Program must command respect and support from all business functions.

3. Program must be supported with long-run commitment.
—May have to evaluate several opportunities before finding success.
—There is a continuing need for new products after initial success.

4. Investigators must be given adequate time for research before decisions are required.
—Shortcuts invite either disaster or missed profits.

5. Investigators must not be distracted by day-to-day business emergencies—they must not be pulled off job to "put out fires."

Figure 13.1

selection, evaluation, and guidance functions, rather than to the technical research (R&D) activities involved, although the R&D function is the beneficiary of the proper organization and guidance procedures discussed.

Full Support of the CEO or COO

First, and foremost, the new product program must have the full support of the chief executive officer (CEO) or chief operating officer (COO), or director of the unit involved, *regardless* of the organizational form or reporting position within the unit. There are two major reasons for this. First, the product activities are a primary means by which the organization takes the necessary steps or changes in direction in order to reach the firm's (or division's) intermediate and long-term objectives. And presumably the objectives are (or should be) a reflection of top management's view of where the unit is heading and how fast it should be moving.

Second, the new product activity needs the full support of the CEO or COO if the project is going to receive the necessary support (financial and otherwise) from other business functions or departments as the evaluation and development sequences proceed.

Respect and Support of Other Business Functions

The second general requirement for success shown in Figure 13.1 is that the new product program must command respect and support (including manpower) from all other business functions involved. The reason is that the new product function must have help and cooperation from the related functions in writing hypotheses and in conducting the necessary investigations. For example, it may be necessary to have an engineer travel with the new product investigator on some of the exploratory and qualitative interviews in order to have a correct assessment made of technical requirements.

Long-Run Commitment Needed

The third general requirement for success shown in Figure 13.1 is that the new product program be supported with a long-run commitment—of funds and personnel. If a formal new product program is being established for the first time, a number of potential opportunities may have to be evaluated before success is achieved. And, even if success is achieved within a reasonable period of time, the new product activity should not be discontinued. As is indicated in the figure, every firm must consider its new product activities a continuing business function just like the accounting function, the production control function, etc. No gain is permanent. Every product has a life cycle, whose length depends heavily on competitive product offerings.

The *level* of new product activities may have to change to meet conditions. But the surest way of avoiding a crisis approach to new product development is to maintain a steady program year after year, with adequate funding.

Once a new product development program has been established, there are two common pitfalls to avoid in its operation. The procedural requirements designed to avoid these pitfalls are shown as numbers 4 and 5 in Figure 13.1.

Shortcuts Lead to Disaster or Missed Profits

There is always pressure to speed up the research process by shortcutting steps in the procedure, shown as item 4 in the figure. The reader will recall the amount of information shown in earlier chapters required to evaluate an opportunity and to understand the need in sufficient depth to guide the technical product development. A firm which has historically "flown by the seat of its pants" in new product developments tends to become impatient with the time and effort required to implement the procedures described earlier. Very commonly, midway in the process, comments will be heard such as, "Why can't we get on with the development now? We already have more information than we have ever had on any other product."

At the end of the qualitative phase this sentiment can be very strong. But, as we pointed out earlier, there are important items of information missing, concerning the size of market segments and competitive penetration, which are obtained in the quantitative stage. Nevertheless, the authors have observed a number of instances where firms have moved ahead with the new product development and market introduction without completing the quantitative phase. And in every instance, the executives involved admitted later that it was a mistake to have done so.

The typical result is that the initial growth in sales is disappointing, and efforts must be made to find out why and correct the situation. The logical step is to conduct a quantitative survey as quickly as possible and to reassess the product and marketing program. All the while the "clock is running" and opportunity costs are rising. When appropriate adjustments are made, the sales rise as expected, but field changes in products are expensive and competition has had more time to react. All the time and effort lost eventually adds up to missed profits.

New Product Efforts Must Not Be Diverted by Day-to-Day Emergencies

The fifth general requirement (to avoid the second pitfall) shown in Figure 13.1 is that new product personnel not be distracted from performing the new product activities. Diversions of their effort typically occur for two reasons. First, the new product investigations are long-range in nature, leading to the (wrong) conclusion that therefore it won't hurt to postpone the activity "just a little while longer." Second, the personnel likely to be involved in the new product work are highly qualified, often with both technical and marketing education and experience. Thus, when an unexpected problem arises with one of the firm's major customers, who is just the right person to handle the problem? Yes, the director of new products, or a member of his staff who certainly can postpone his or her long-range work for a few days (or weeks). So it is reasoned. The problem is that the person often *is* the one most qualified to handle the emergency, but if such a person is assigned that responsibility, even infrequently, the new product activity loses its momentum. With these five general requirements for success as background, we next examine the requirements for communication and review.

General Requirements for Communication and Review

Successful new product development requires the blending and analysis of a great deal of information from diverse sources. Several functional departments, each with different views and objectives, are involved. Success with new product development depends directly on the communication and coordination among the various units involved. The requirements for communication and review have been condensed into four basic "musts," shown in Figure 13.2. The requirements are independent of the method of organization employed.

1. Provide Timely Communication with All Involved

The first and key requirement is that the director of the new product activity keep all other related business functions informed (including the CEO, COO, or Director) as information in the new product investigation is developed. There are two important aspects of this requirement. First, the responsibility for obtaining the review and communication should be *fixed* and fixed with the person responsible for the new product function. Second, communication should be maintained with other related units *as the*

1. Director and staff must keep all other business functions informed as information is developed.
   —No function should be left in the dark.
   —No surprises.

2. All related business functions must have chance to review results periodically and question them as information is developed.

3. All related business functions must be made to feel part of the final decision.
   —They should not have to accept decision of another department.

4. New product director and staff must aid other business functions in correctly perceiving product-marketing-manufacturing requirements in order to perform their part of the total task properly.

Figure 13.2

information is developed. This means that weekly or biweekly trip reports and memos should be sent to closely related functions, and there should be no doubt about who prepares and circulates these reports. Initially, close communication will be needed with R&D and marketing, and later (or when requested) with manufacturing and finance. Review meetings should be organized at the conclusion of predetermined phases, such as at the completion of screening, exploratory, qualitative, and quantitative phases, or at stages of accomplishments such as completion of first prototype, etc. It is important that no key management personnel or related business function be "left in the dark" as the investigation and development proceeds. Furthermore, no one should be surprised or handed a "fait accompli" at the end.

2. Provide Opportunity to Review and Question

The second basic requirement shown in Figure 13.2 is that all related business functions have an opportunity to review results periodically and question them as information is being gathered and analyzed. This is closely related to the first requirement above.

The emphasis here, however, is on the opportunity for *input* from the related business units, not merely on their being kept informed as emphasized in the first requirement.

The opportunity for input from other units accomplishes two major things. First, it improves and increases the efficiency of the research process by making maximum use of the in-house knowledge to help guide and direct the research activity. It helps assure that the correct issues are addressed and the best sources of information are reached. The researcher should avoid at all costs reactions such as, "Why didn't you ask our department? We could have told you that technology wasn't suitable," or "Those were not the right people to see about that issue," etc.

The second thing accomplished by periodic input from related units is the fostering of a climate of cooperation and objective openmindedness. This helps departments with diverse objectives to work together better toward a common company objective. In turn it leads toward accomplishing the third requirement.

3. Involve All Departments in Final Decision

The third general requirement for communication and review is that all business units be made to feel a part of the final decision (concerning whether to go ahead with the product, which features it should have, etc.). It is most important that no department, such as marketing, be required to accept the decisions of another department, such as R&D. The decision should be made jointly, with input to each area based on solid objective facts obtained by the new product function.

As the reader can probably sense by now, the overriding requirement for success in new product development is a climate of amicable, voluntary, open cooperation among the diverse departments involved. The reason is that each department involved (except the new product department itself) has its own major tasks to perform. New product activities must be done "in addition to" the normal, everyday departmental activities. It is not without justification that new product activities have been said to be "disruptive" of normal business activities.

Given this basic character, perhaps it can be more readily understood why the proper cooperative climate is so valuable. It is not that new product development cannot be done at all; it is simply that a noncooperative or hostile environment leads to inefficiencies which compound the costs involved.

4. Assure Continuity and Follow-through to Market

The fourth general requirement for communication and review is that those involved with the new product activity aid the related functions, especially manufacturing and marketing, in correctly perceiving the product-marketing requirements in order that these units can correctly perform their own tasks. There are two reasons for this requirement: (1) the long time span typical of new product developments, and (2) the risks inherent in new product introductions.

a. *Continuity Needs Over Long Time Spans*

After months, or years, in the development process, key personnel often have been transferred or promoted. In designing the product for production at a later stage, no one may be around who knows *why* certain features or materials are essential to meet the market requirements. Out of ignorance, costly mistakes can be made. These mistakes can be avoided if those involved with the new product function continue to monitor the product throughout the subsequent stages until market introduction. For example, a person from the new product department can be made a member of the manufacturing and marketing committees responsible for the product.

b. *Avoid Mistakes in Market Introduction*

The reader will recall our earlier discussion of the elements of a marketing strategy: the specification of the target market, and product, price, promotion, and place channels. In the process of researching the product requirements, those responsible for the new product identify the target market and obtain information concerning price as well as product. A good deal of information is also obtained concerning the promotional and distribution needs. All this information should be used in designing the marketing strategy. Thus, those involved with the new product should communicate this information to the marketing department and assist in the development of the strategy.

Often a market test is needed to verify key strategy elements. Here again, those involved with the new product activity have information to provide assistance. Problems with new product introductions are a significant source of missed profits. A lack of follow-through from development to market introduction is often

208

cited as a major source of difficulty. Improving and assuring communication as described above, can be an effective means of minimizing the problem.

Organizational Options and Level of Staffing

There is probably more diversity in the organization of new product development activities than in the organization of any other business function. This reflects the multifaceted nature of the function as well as its early stage of development as a recognized business function. For these reasons, it is recommended above all else that the organization be kept *flexible*. This is no place for rigid procedures or protocols.

Among the various options available, we have seen two consistently achieve success in the development of products within the scope of the existing markets, technologies, and methods of manufacture. These include (1) the separate new product department, and (2) the project team.

We have also seen the venture team concept succeed in the development of new products completely outside the scope of the existing business. Additionally, new products are sometimes obtained through licensing and acquisition of other firms. Providing guidance for such licensings and acquisitions and assisting with the evaluation of associated new product opportunities are important aspects of the new product function. For this reason, as we indicated earlier in Chapter 4, when restating objectives, it is important to clarify to what extent new products should be obtained internally or externally. This issue must be reexamined periodically as market and competitive conditions change.

The New Product Department

Depending on the size of the firm and the nature of the business, new product departments may consist solely of a director and a secretary; or a director, secretary, and one or several assistants; or a director, secretary, and a staff of assistants and specialists in technical areas, markets, government regulations, standards, etc. One person and a secretary is sufficient for a small firm or division with sales up to about $25 million. Beyond that, an assistant is needed for approximately each additional 25 to 50 million dollars in sales. Thus, a firm or division with sales of 75 to 125 million dollars will usually require a director and one or two assistants.

Corporate new product departments are usually more thinly staffed per million dollars of sales than divisional departments because projects are often taken over by divisions after preliminary evaluation and development at the corporate level. Often, the size of the corporate staff depends largely on the number of technical specialties which need representation. New product departments at all organizational levels interface continually with the technical product development activities (R&D), but rarely include the technical development work within the new product department itself.

The normal scope of new product department functions thus includes establishing screening criteria, stimulation of and searching for new product ideas, evaluating and shaping new product opportunities, and guiding and coordinating the development and market introduction activities. Each stage of the screening and evaluative activities is done in consultation with the most expert personnel in the line departments affected (marketing, R&D, etc.). We recommend that the work of the new product department itself be guided and reviewed by a high-level management committee representing the various departments involved and chaired by the CEO, COO, or Director himself. This committee should assure that adequate budget is available to the new product department as well as to other departments that must provide expert assistance.

Where no formal new product activity is recognized or staffed within a firm or division, the new product activity is often performed in a creative research and engineering or marketing department, or is spread between the two.

This may be necessary when a firm is first established, or in a small division. However, if no provision is made to formally organize and staff the new product function after the firm or division reaches about $10 million in sales, the new product development function usually loses its efficiency. Such firms also tend to lose their sense of direction at about this size, compounding the errors in new product development. Thus, it is at about this size that objectives also need to be restated and new product screening criteria established to provide the guidance for new product activities. We have successfully established new product programs in firms with sales as low as $3.5 million.

The Project Team

The project team concept was initially devised as a technique for coordinating and expediting the development of military products. The emphasis of the approach was to assemble a team of managerial and technical experts who could expedite an urgently needed development toward a clearly defined objective, often working outside established channels. The original concept has been modified to provide guidance and coordination for routine new product developments. The result is a matrix-like structure. Personnel from different disciplines (marketing, engineering, production design, manufacturing, quality conrol, etc.) are assigned to the team as part of their total job. Each person may serve on several new product project teams. One person is assigned responsibility for the team's work. This may be a full-time or part-time assignment.

If no formal new product department exists, (which is usually the case where this technique is used), the team leader is usually from marketing or engineering. If a separate new product function exists, it is logical to appoint a member of that department to head the team. If this is the case, the operation becomes very much like that described for the new product department above, but with the roles of various team members more clearly defined.

The Venture Team

In contrast with project teams whose focus in new product development is usually on similar products for familiar markets, the venture team is designed to take the firm into an entirely different market, usually with a new product as well.[6] The diversification effort of Lear Siegler's Instrument Division, from its traditional military-electronics business into materials handling in the office environment with the Mailmobile[R] vehicle is a classic example. The venture team, whose multidisciplinary members usually represent all major business functions, is established as a separate operation with its own budget, usually reporting to the CEO, COO, or Director. However, it can also report to another executive, including the head of R&D.[7] The team is given a general objective such as that shown in Chapter 6 for the Mailmobile[R] system.

The team searches for ideas, conducts the screening, and with the consent of the COO or new product committee at each stage, proceeds all the way through evaluation, development, manufacture and market introduction. Assistance may be obtained from the firm or purchased outside for the technical and manufacturing development. The team is given a budget for these activities and has responsibility for getting the work done, whether externally or internally.

Within the Specialty Materials Group of AMF, the Group Executive established a "Venture Division" reporting to him as do other division presidents. This future new division was staffed with a skeleton crew of key functional managers and given the mission to start a new business within certain broad guidelines via any route they chose: new product spinoff from existing units, new product development, or acquisition. A budget and time frame were also established.

After the new product is launched, the venture team members usually continue with the new business venture as operating executives in the major functional departments, as intended in the AMF example above.

Reporting Level and Review Committees

We strongly recommend that the new product function report directly to the CEO, COO, or Director as shown in Figure 13.3 regardless of the oganizational form used. We further recommend, as shall be elaborated later, that the vice president (or managers) of the principal functional elements shown (R&D, Marketing, Manufacturing, and Finance) together with the COO, serve as members of the new products committee to provide direction and coordination of the new product development activity.

Where it is desirable to have new product development activities at both the divisional and group or corporate levels, we again recommend that the new product function report to the respective COO's as illustrated in Figure 13.4, with coordination maintained between the new product directors at each level.

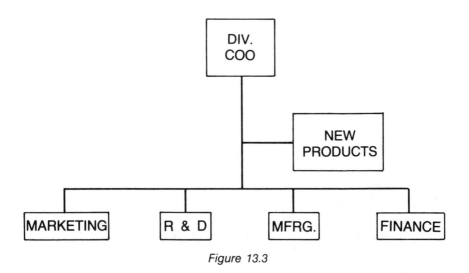

REPORTING TO COO

Figure 13.3

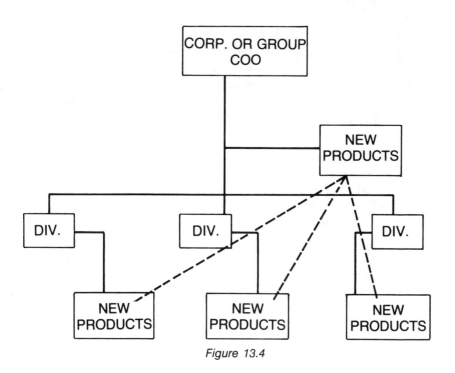

CORPORATE OR GROUP AND DIVISIONAL LEVEL

Figure 13.4

Reporting to R&D or Marketing

Although we strongly recommend that the new product function be positioned so it reports directly to the COO, we do not mean to imply that it cannot work well when reporting to the managers of R&D or marketing, the two logical alternatives. With exceptionally capable executives in either position, the new product activity can be successful. Even when this is the case, however, it takes a greater effort to make the process work, especially to achieve the necessary cooperation and assistance from related functions.

Either of these organizational options is easier to implement if the firm (or division) is relatively small, and lines of communication are short and informal. For these reasons, either option can make sense in a new startup situation. In such instances, if a high-technology product is involved, it usually is more logical to have the function report to R&D. On the other hand, if little technical sophistication is required, or strong emotive elements of need are involved, such as with consumer products, having the new product activity report to marketing is normally the more suitable option. Of couse, problems may occur in either case if the firm becomes a large unit and the new product activity has not been formalized and staffed as discussed earlier.

When the volume of new product activities associated with multiple product lines becomes too large to direct and coordinate with a single effort reporting to the COO, multilevel new product activities are appropriate, as shown in Figure 13.5. Firms or divisions with sales approaching $100 million typically require this type of organization. In this mode, responsibility for new product activities associated with modifications and logical extensions of existing products is delegated to the product managers, while the responsibility for long-range new product programs is fixed with the new product director who reports directly to the COO. A good deal of coordination is required with multilevel new product activities, as shown in the figure, to assure that no overlaps of activity or gaps in coverage occur as a result of the separate activities. However, we have observed consistent success with this organizational mode in large firms.

MULTIPLE FUNCTIONS AT DIFFERENT LEVELS

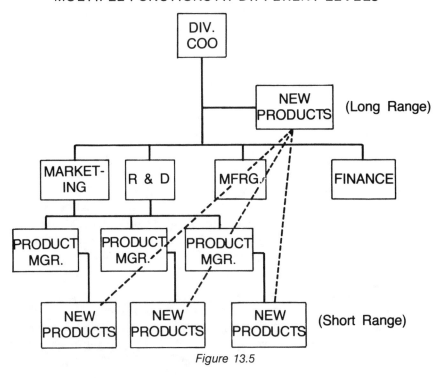

Figure 13.5

The New Products Committee

Although there have been many well-justified criticisms of committees; e.g., "a camel is a horse designed by a committee," there are important roles for one or more committees in new product development activities. Within the procedural framework advocated in the above chapters, one or more committees can be very useful in at least two roles: (1) to provide guidance for the new product work, and (2) to provide communication between the new product function and the related business units.

Unless the firm or division is very large with many product lines, the guidance, review, and communication can be provided by one committee. This committee is ideally composed of the CEO, COO or director (hereafter only called COO), and the vice

215

presidents or managers of the related business functions, usually R&D, marketing, manufacturing, and finance, and often quality control and engineering as well. The COO serves as chairman of the committee, and the director of the new product function serves as the executive staff for the committee. The new product director essentially does the preparation for the meetings. He usually organizes the meetings and sets the agenda with the advice and approval of the chairman.

In their decision-making role, the committee members actually serve as advisors to the COO. Thus, when the committee makes a decision, it is actually the COO making the decision, with the advice of his first-line officers. In this role the committee reviews the work of the new product activity at each stage in the procedure. It makes decisions regarding the adequacy of the research and whether or not the results justify continuation, and establishes priorities among projects. The committee also reviews and approves the budget necessary for the conduct of the new product investigations, including the support necessary from each of the departments represented on the committee.

In its comunication role, the committee channels information concerning new product programs back to personnel in each of the departments sooner or later to be affected. The committee members also provide suggestions to the new product director concerning sources of information, both within and outside the firm, as well as suggestions from others. Once a program of investigation is established, most of the communication between the new product activity and other related departments is done directly. The committee merely facilitates the direct working relationships.

More Than One Committee is Needed
In Large Firms

Where the size of the firm and number of product lines is quite large, one new product committee may not be able to handle the total job. In such a case, new product activities would probably be organized at multiple levels, such as shown previously in Figure 13.5. (Recall in that instance that new product activities were divided on the basis of long- and short-range developmens.) In such

216

a case, the long-range activities would be guided and reviewed by the new products committee just described. The shorter-range activities might have a separate new products committee for the same purpose (or possibly several committees), but staffed by second-level managers in the departments involved. In this case, the two (or more) committees should meet several times a year as a commitee of the whole to coordinate the total new product program.

Personnel Qualifications

Although proper organization and procedures are important in new product development, nothing is more important than the personnel chosen for this work. After working in the field and teaching engineering and business students for many years, we have gained considerable insight into the personnel qualifications for the new product function. Here we are speaking of the director of the function and his staff who would normally report to the CEO or COO. They would be responsible for the development and maintenance of the screening criteria, the initial screening of new products, the evaluation and investigation of new opportunities (including the direction of the work of outside market research firms), and the communication and coordination activities up to market introduction. A summary of the qualifications for this work is shown in Figure 13.6.

On occasion, when we are explaining the qualifications for this type of work to an executive for the first time, we have been told something like, "Why don't you add the requirement that the person be able to walk on water, as well; you have everything else." It seems this way, but it must be recognized that these are ideal requirements. If the new product function has only a director and secretary, the director must meet the requirements as nearly as possible. However, if several persons are involved in the activity, the skills can be distributed among them, especially regarding education.

Note in Figure 13.6 that we recommend the combination of a bachelor's degree in engineering or other appropriate technical field (such as food science in the Figurines[R] case in Chapter 12)

PERSONNEL QUALIFICATIONS FOR
NEW PRODUCTS FUNCTION

Education

Bachelor's degree in engineering or other appropriate technical field, and some training in business, such as MBA.

Experience

A minimum of several years in an engineering or technical position, *and* several years in marketing or position requiring customer contact.

Stature

Able to command respect and credibility from the COO and all functional managers, both technical and nontechnical.

Intellectual Characteristics

—Logical, open-minded, realistic
—Analytical, objective evaluator
—Critical, questioning mind
—Creative and innovative outlook

Emotional Characteristics

—Ability to disdain the advocacy role for particular products
—Self-motivated, conscious of time
—Positive outlook; emotionally stable
—Capable of finding new approach when things go wrong
—Strength of purpose to keep digging to get correct answers
—Ability to be satisfied with the right answer even if it is not the popular one

Interpersonal Skills

—Excellent diplomatic skills
—Tact, nonabrasiveness
—Good communication skills (verbal and written) with technical and nontechnical persons
—Ability to work in harmony with co-workers

Skills in Planning, Managing, and Directing

—Good advance planner, ability to visualize all steps required in future activities
—Ability to make efficient use of minimal resources
—Ability to coordinate multiple activities
—Appreciation of importance of attention to detail

Figure 13.6

and training in business, such as an MBA. A minimum of several years experience in engineering or other technical field is desired *as well as* in marketing or other customer-contact work.

The reason these qualifications are necessary is that the personnel must be able to understand all aspects of need: physical (including emotive), economic, and technical. If the staff is larger than a single director, persons with different qualifications may complement each other, as we have already mentioned. However, this seems to work well only in very large departments or where the project team concept is used.

We have often observed, when using class projects to teach new product development, that MBA students with a nontechnical background often cannot determine the physical requirements for a new product in sufficient depth, simply because they cannot communicate in the technical language needed. On the other hand, MBA students with an engineering background in the same class have been very successful in doing so, and in assisting others to do so when working together in teams. We have observed the same to be true in working with personnel in industry.

In smaller new products departments individuals are usually given total responsibility for one or more new product projects. When the new product function is initially formulated in a company, it usually starts with one person who has the multidisciplinary background described in the figure. And even in a large department it is very important that the director of the function have such multidisciplinary education and experience.

It is also essential that the director of the activity have considerable stature within the company as indicated in the figure. This is also desirable for all members of the new product staff, but it is *essential* for the director. He or she must have the complete confidence of the COO and the respect and cooperation of all functional managers. The position should be considered no lower than one position below a functional unit vice president, such as vice president of R&D or marketing. These executives normally serve on the new products review committee to provide guidance and review of the new product work. The director should therefore have considerable stature in the eyes of these committee members.

The intellectual characteristics needed by new products personnel include a logical, analytic, objective, open-minded, and creative outlook. Such people also must be self-motivated and emotionally stable. They must be able to function without assuming an advocacy role on favorite new products. To do so will destroy the objectivity needed, and most likely lead to bias in the evaluation. We have observed several instances where this has occurred. The typical result is that important facts are overlooked or not given appropriate weight in the decision process. In either case, the credibility of the new-product program is likely to be severely damaged.

The new products staff must have sufficient emotional security to be satisifed by determining the *correct* answer, whether or not it is the *popular* one as well. The new product director need not take a position on whether a particular opportunity should or should not be pursued. He and his staff are responsible for framing the hypotheses and obtaining the information necessary to test them properly. Of course, in both cases, he obtains help from others within the company to do so. Once the proper information has been collected and organized, the decision makers, the CEO or COO and the new product committee, should make the necessary decision.

Interpersonal skills in diplomacy, tact, and communications are absolutely essential for this type of work. A tactful, non-abrasive approach is necessary to obtain the much-needed assistance from others at various stages of development.

Since there is a great deal of communication involved, the director and staff must be able to comunicate effectively, both orally and in writing, and with a diversity of people. For example, on a given product investigation it might be necessary to communicate with executives of customer firms, with machine operators, with servicemen, and with engineers and other technical personnel. Here again we have observed that personnel without an engineering or technical background are greatly handicapped in studying the requirements for most industrial/commercial products. They simply cannot communicate at the technical level well enough to understand the physical and technical requirements.

Both the director and staff should be good advance planners to assure that all the needed evaluation and coordination is available at the correct time in the development sequence. In both evaluation and coordination activities, personnel should give particular attention to detail. This is no job for a "big picture type" who has disdain for detail.

And finally the director and staff should also have the ability to make efficient use of time and scarce resources, and appreciate their importance. The key to success in new product activities is not "empire building" but in efficient use of just the right amount of the right resource at the right time with a "lean and mean" crew for the coordination and evaluation functions.

Summary

We have shown that there are a number of organizational, procedural, and communications matters which affect the success of new product developments. Based on our experiences, we have presented a series of recommendations regarding each of these areas. It is especially important that the function have the full support of the COO, and that a climate of open communication and cooperation exist among all departments involved.

We have also described several organizational options we have found to be successful for the new product function, including creation of a separate department, project teams, and the venture team concept. We have also addressed issues concerning whom the new product activity should report to and the levels at which the function should be established in company organizations. Lastly, we have described personnel qualifications for the director and staff of the new product function. In doing so, we have indicated the need for a multidisciplinary background and for other intellectual and emotional characteristics and interpersonal skills.

Footnotes to Chapter 13

[1]Richard N. Foster, "Organize for Technology Transfer," *Harvard Business Review* (November-December, 1971), pp. 110–19.

[2]Jay W. Lorsch and Paul R. Lawrence, "Organizing for Product Innovation," *Harvard Business Review* Vol. 43 (January–February, 1965), pp. 109–22.

³James E. Stafford and James U. McNeal, "Organizing for Product Planning," *Advanced Management Journal*, Vol. 29 No. 1 (January, 1964), pp. 28–33.

⁴Richard F. Vancil, "Better Management of Corporate Development," *Harvard Business Review*, Vol. 50, No. 5 (September–October, 1972), pp. 53–62.

⁵Davis S. Hopkins, *Options in New-Product Organization* (The Conference Board, Inc., 1974).

⁶Richard M. Hill and James D. Hlavacek, "The Venture Team: A New Concept in Marketing Organization," *Journal of Marketing*, Vol. 36 (July, 1972), pp. 44–50.

⁷Warren R. Stumpe, "Venture Management is Part of R&D," *Research/Development* (November, 1976), pp. 32–40.

Chapter 14

Summary and Conclusion: A Better Method is Possible

We began by explaining that problems with new product development stem from the accelerating pace of technological change and the tacit acceptance of three popular myths.

The myth of "a better mousetrap" is misleading in that it encourages invention without understanding of user need and the importance of other marketing elements. The myth of "another Xerox" misdirects attention toward improbable great inventions or technical breakthroughs instead of toward a series of modest advances which history has shown to be the more likely route to significant technical and commercial success. And the myth of the "gift of genius" misleads by suggesting that new products come only from a flash of genius rather than from systematic analysis and dedicated research.

We then proceeded to show that there were three keys to the dissolution of the myths and to the solution of most problems with the new product development process. These keys are to obtain in-depth understanding of market needs before technical development; to focus on innovation instead of invention; and to use systematic and efficient procedures throughout the new product development process.

In moving toward the development of more operational procedures, we expanded the three keys into an expression of the philosophy of our approach as five essential ingredients for successful innovation:

1. Shift to marketing orientation.
2. Choose opportunities which match resources.
3. Develop proper screening criteria.
4. Conduct requirements research in sufficient depth before technical development.
5. Organize, staff, and fund adequately for long-run success.

Finally, we have shown how the ingredients in our philosophy can be converted into practical procedures which produce successful results. These procedures were explained in the remaining chapters grouped into two sections according to strategic and new product procedures. These procedures are shown together in Figure 14.1.

Why Success is Assured

It has been our experience that whenever the strategic and new product procedures outlined in Figure 14.1 and explained in the above chapters are followed to a reasonable degree, success with new product developments is virtually assured. This is a strong statement. We have confidence in making it, however, because the procedures we have devised and recommend above do more than merely *evaluate* new product opportunities. The procedures are also designed to *guide* and *shape* the initial opportunity into a form which *can be* successful.

Of course, if there is very little chance for any kind of success, as, for example, because of an improper matching of resources or inadequate market size, the procedures will quickly disclose that as well. In this way the procedures assure overall success by preventing the costly mistakes of spending time and resources on opportunities that must be abandoned later. For example, when asked to appear as a speaker at one of our seminars, an executive of a small firm which had been using our procedures for five or six years replied in an almost embarrassed tone that he didn't have any great successes to talk about. He went on to say that all our procedures had done was to prevent him from making mistakes with proposed new products. As a result, the company had continued to modify and improve its existing products and apply them in new markets. The result was a tripling in sales and profits over the period.

Through results such as this, we are confident that our procedures have sucessfully addressed the major causes of new product failure. But we are not so naive as to believe that nothing can go wrong. We have seen Murphy's Law alive and active in many of the developments with which we have been associated. We shall close by pointing out some major pitfalls which have occurred

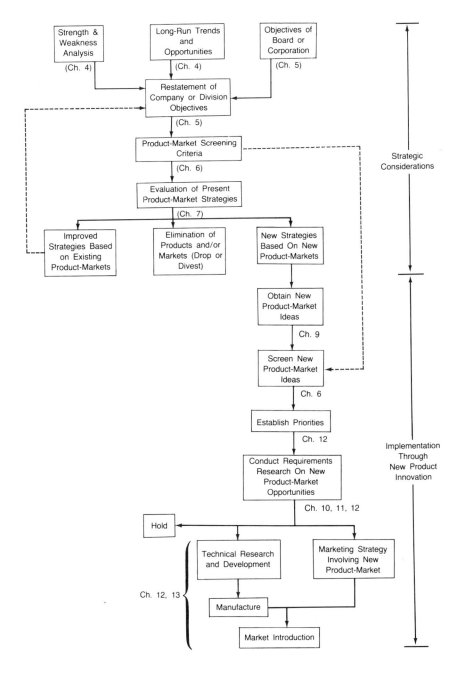

Figure 14.1   Overview of Planned Innovation Procedures.

225

even when everything was supposedly done "according to Hoyle," or should we say, "according to Bacon and Butler."

What Can Still Go Wrong

Of course anything that can go wrong, will. With this concept in mind we have chosen nine sources of trouble for you to beware of, even when everything seems to be going well. These are summarized in Figure 14.2 and discussed below.

Transfer of Knowledge to Sales and Manufacture

People who have lived with a new product development for three to five years often do not realize how much information has been obtained, and what elements are essential if those who are to carry on the marketing and production are to be successful. There is a great tendency to feel that things are obvious, when they definitely are not obvious to others.

For example, when Toledo Scale developed the first electronic digital parts counter, (shown earlier in Figure 10.3), the sales organization assumed that it was a replacement for the existing mechanical parts-counting scales. This was a logical assumption because in the few years preceding, Toledo Scale had developed

---

WHERE THINGS GO WRONG

1. Transfer of knowledge to sales and manufacture.
2. Coordination of sales and distribution with production buildup.
3. Inadequate marketing support.
4. Misunderstanding of product usage or features by potential customers.
5. Unanticipated environmental conditions or regulations.
6. Misuse of product, and unanticipated product liability.
7. Product failure and missing parts.
8. Inability to produce due to unavailability of critical components or materials.
9. Unanticipated escalation of costs.

Figure 14.2

and very successfully marketed an electronic scale for grocery stores and supermarkets (shown earlier in Figure 10.4) to replace the (then) existing mechanical-optical scale.

On the other hand, the new electronic parts-counting scale was intended for an entirely different target market than was its mechanical predecessor. This was because the electronic scale, being slightly less accurate, but much faster in operation, could be used for counting inexpensive parts which never would have been considered on the mechanical scale because of the high labor cost of doing so. Thus, the new scale had many applications in receiving, shipping, and in-process inventory control, which had never been feasible for the mechanical scale. Strange as it may seem, in the beginning this message was not effectively communicated to the sales organization, with the result that initial marketing efforts missed the target market.

Similar stories can be told regarding transfer of information to manufacturing. Here it is often the critical nature of certain components, materials, or tolerances that is not effectively communicated. Because of effort to manufacture at minimum costs, substitutions occur which degrade the performance of the product.

Coordination of Sales and Distribution With Production Buildup

People frequently argue about which case is worse: not having product when and where you need it to get orders, or having a large inventory buildup and not enough orders to move it. There is no doubt, however, that success depends on avoiding both situations.

Closely related to these problems is not having spare parts available when and where they are needed, or support service capability. When entering a new market, coordinating the establishment of sales and service organizations in different geographical regions can be a perplexing problem.

For example, in first introducing the Mailmobile[R] system (Chapter 6), Lear Siegler was faced with the problem that it was not economical to establish a service capability in an area until the sales had reached an appropriate level. Because they wished to service the product themselves to protect proprietary interests, to get feedback on product performance, and to insure excellent

227

service to initial customers, they did not want to contract the service to a third party. Yet, with such a new and untried product, customers insisted on service availability as a condition of purchase. It is in such situations that venture managers earn their salary (and get a few more gray hairs).

Inadequate Marketing Support

Successful product launch can become stymied if potential customers do not find out about the product or if sales efforts are ineffective in obtaining orders. Such problems can occur for a variety of reasons: advertisements and promotional materials that do not emphasize differentiating product features (or stress the wrong ones), improper choice of media or channels of distribution, inadequately trained sales personnel, etc. The list can go on and on. Of course, many of the problems could be avoided by proper use of the procedures we recommend, or of other sound marketing principles.[1]

Inadequate marketing support often occurs when a firm enters a new market with a new distribution channel. For example, when the small Mayfair Marine Company of Troy, Michigan, introduced its unique folding boat ladder to the marine industry it did so through established channels.[2] However, being unfamiliar with the industry, the management had no way to identify the "good" reps, distributors, and dealers in different regions of the country. It was only after a series of somewhat bitter and disappointing experiences that they were able to locate effective channel members and achieve the sales levels anticipated.

Misunderstanding of Product Usage or Features by Potential Customers

When the new product is really different from the existing ones, there exists a large chance that it will be misunderstood by potential customers. This was true of the electronic parts-counting scale mentioned above, where its use was even misunderstood by some people in the firm which developed it.

It was especially true of the Mailmobile[R] vehicle when it was introduced, because no product had ever existed for automatically delivering mail and office supplies from desk to desk within the office environment. The initial problem faced in marketing the equipment was to convince customers that it was a realistic option. Many potential customers initially perceived it as a fascinating toy rather than a money-saving item of capital equipment.

When Mayfair Marine developed its folding boat ladder it found that an ideal material for the ladder was "structural foam," a polyethelene plastic developed by Union Carbide for automobile batteries. The material proved to be very strong, impervious to deterioration or corrosion in fresh or salt water, and to top things off, it could be formulated with a specific gravity less than that of water so that the ladder would float if inadvertently dropped overboard. Early news releases and promotional materials stressed the use of the new "structural foam" material and the ladder's ability to float,[3] as shown in Figure 14.3.

Unfortunately, the material was unknown to the general public. Thus, when they learned the ladder could float, the public assumed it was a "styra-foam" ladder, which obviously could not be very durable.

This significantly hampered the acceptance of the new product. In order to overcome the problem the company had the ladder tested by an independent agency, (which certified its weight-carrying capacity to be over 500 pounds) and then offered a one-year unconditional warranty on the product. The warranty was very effective in overcoming the misconception, but valuable time and money were consumed in the corrective action. Later promotional materials stressed the ladder's folding-stowable properties and deemphasized the material used (see Figure 14.4). The problem could have been avoided had the advertisements been tested with a consumer central location test or a market test, as was done by Pillsbury with Figurines[R]. But managers of small companies seldom feel they have resources for such tests and usually opt to take the greater risk.

Unanticipated Environmental Conditions or Regulations

Even with the most thorough research of product requirements, environmental conditions which affect product performance may not be discovered until the product is in use. Although aware of the fact that factory environments were hostile

STEP UP TO MAYFAIR
Structural Foam Boat Ladder

3.3 square

43.75

BIA

Pat. Appl. For.

STOWABLE — Folds completely and compactly for easy stowage in narrow spaces.

FEATURES

1. **UNIVERSAL**—Can be quickly fitted to any boat, runabout, cruiser, sailboat, or pontoon; adaptable to any gunnel or deck condition.

2. **EXCEPTIONALLY SAFE**—Completely secure and stable when snapped into the permanent deck latches; cannot slip overboard.

3. **ENGINEERED** — Total design concept provides best possible climbing angle, eliminates abrasion or marking of the hull and interior trim, does not interfere with gunnel hand rails or tracks, and gives the user a feeling of security because of its firmness and stability.

4. **ATTRACTIVE COLOR**—The white color and slim functional appearance belie its rugged strength and durability.

5. **FLOATS** — Guaranteed to float on top of the water, where its white color can be easily seen.

6. **GUARANTEED** — With each ladder, there is a two-year written guarantee from the manufacturer against breakage.

7. **NO MAINTENANCE** — Structural foam is virtually maintenance free.

8. **HARDWARE**—Each ladder comes complete and ready for mounting. No extras to buy!

STRUCTURAL FOAM

The **MAYFAIR BOAT LADDER** is manufactured from structural foam, a new material processed by Union Carbide. Something new in plastics, tough enough to take the worst abuse and yet light enough in weight to float. This material, which is noncorrosive, highly resistant to marine growth, and molded in colors, has a great future in the marine industry. Watch for more exciting products of structural foam from

Figure 14.3 Early Promotional Material for Mayfair Marine's Folding Boat Ladder.

230

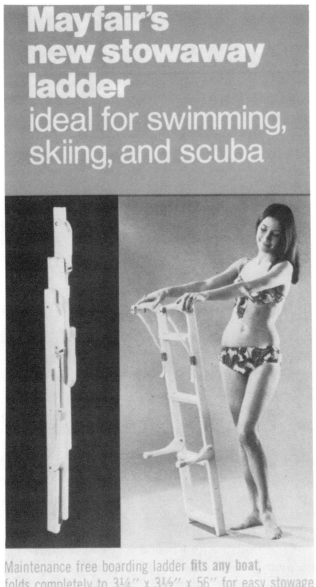

Mayfair's new stowaway ladder
ideal for swimming, skiing, and scuba

Maintenance free boarding ladder fits any boat, folds completely to 3¼" x 3½" x 56" for easy stowage

A totally new concept in boarding ladders is the Mayfair boat ladder which can be easily mounted to any gunnel or deck condition. Made from "structural foam," a process created by Union Carbide, this patented ladder has amazing strength—capable of supporting in excess of 500 pounds—yet it floats.

—Arbor Advertising, Ann Arbor, Michigan

Figure 14.4 Later Promotional Material for Mayfair Marine's Folding Boat Ladder.

environments for electronic computers, early developers of numerical controls for machine tools received some rude shocks. In one case a numerically controlled gear cutter could not be made to perform reliably. After much study it was discovered that large voltage spikes were coming into the power line from electric welding equipment that was occasionally operated nearby, without an isolation transformer.

In some applications of the Mailmobile[R] system, it was discovered that optical brighteners used in some carpet shampoos left a fluorescent residue which affected the photo-optical guidance system. Furthermore, it was found that New York City had special codes requiring that all electrical/electronic equipment have a U.L. listing, thereby requiring the listing for the Mailmobile[R] vehicles, although most of the cities did not have such a requirement.

Misuse of Product and Unanticipated Product Liability

Until recently, many manufacturers felt that if customers chose to misuse equipment, they should bear the consequences. However, with recent tightening of product liability legislation, manufacturers are more concerned that equipment cannot be misused. A case in point is the recent requirement for automatic shutoff of rotary lawn mowers when the operator is not holding the handle.

Occasionally, even though the product is designed to meet the requirements, misuse can result in injury and lawsuit requiring that the product be modified or withdrawn from the market. For example, a manufacturer of some sophisticated medical equipment used with special surgical procedures was sued because the equipment did not function properly, causing injury to a patient, but subsequently learned that the medical technicians had not used the equipment according to instructions. Even though it was not the fault of the manufacturer, experiences like this example can necessitate recall or redesign to prevent similar future misuse.

Product Failure and Missing Parts

Nothing is so infuriating as to buy a new bicycle or garage door opener and find, when attempting to assemble it, that there are a few parts missing. If this were to happen consistently with a new product, such as the AMF bicycles with the new Quick-Shift^R gear-shifting mechanism, it could scuttle an otherwise successful new product launch. Similarly, if the new Quick-Shift^R mechanism should have frequent failures during the first few months of use, the whole effort would be set back greatly, as would be the case with any new product.

In such situations, we apply the "ten to one rule." If consumers or buyers have a negative impression of a new product because of such failures, lack of spare parts, etc., it will take ten times the effort to change their minds about the product as it would have taken to persuade them to buy it in the first place.

Inability to Produce Due to Unavailability of Critical Components or Materials

You might expect that no large firm would plan for market introduction without assuring itself of reliable sources of supply. But it can happen, even to large firms like automobile manufacturers with much experience and sophistication in dealing with supplier firms. In one such case an assembly line was slowed by the lack of foam arm rests, when a historically dependable supplier encountered production problems due to a shipment of contaminated chemicals.

More frequently the problem haunts small firms whose business may not be important to a larger supplier. It happens frequently in periods of materials shortages or periods of rapidly increasing demand for commonly used electronic components.

For example, Mayfair Marine had difficulty obtaining structured foam parts because other firms such as automobile manufacturers began to use the new material.

Unanticipated Escalation in Costs

In today's climate of rampant inflation, there is little likelihood that a builder of large special machine tools, whose construction might require 18 to 24 months, would not include price escalation clauses in the purchase agreement. However, in recent years, some builders failed to include such a clause.

More likely, in today's business climate, problems will result from wide fluctuations in the cost of critical materials, such as gold or silver for relay contacts, or chromium for plating or alloying. Such problems can put an abrupt end to a new product's success, if suitable substitutes are not available.

Summary

Yes, even if correct procedures are followed, there still will be some problems with new product developments. Murphy's Law will see to that. Nevertheless, as the above examples themselves show, most problems can be avoided through intelligent application of the recommended procedures. After all, perhaps we should leave some problems to stimulate and challenge the creativity of management.

Footnotes to Chapter 14

[1]See E. Jerome MacCarthy, *Basic Marketing: A Managerial Approach,* 6th Edition (Homewood, Ill.: Richard D. Irwin, Inc., 978).

[2]See "Troy Company Finalist in State Product Contest," *The Daily Tribune,* Royal Oak, Michigan, May 17, 1971, p. 15. See also *Boating Industry,* June 1974. (The Mayfair line of ladders is now owned by N. A. Taylor Co., Inc., Gloversville, New York.)

[3]*Ibid.*

APPENDIX

THE TECHNICAL BOARD

• *A new management tool*

The Technical Board*

by Frank R. Bacon, Jr. and Thomas W. Butler, Jr.

Business firms increasingly have to deal with problems like the following ones:

A. The chief executive officer of a small instrument firm is studying a proposal from his director of R&D to develop a new spectographic instrument using a plasma-arc energy source. The development offers an opportunity to make a major new market penetration, but the estimated development cost would consume half his R&D budget for two years. He is dealing with a technology new to both his research staff and himself. In order to make the decision, he must be assured that the development is technologically feasible and, if so, that his own organization could make the technical advance necessary. His director of R&D is eager to give it a try, and his sales manager is excited over the prospect of having such a new instrument added to the line.

B. The corporate development officer of a long established medium-sized firm supplying the automotive industry is trying to decide whether his firm should move into powdered metallurgy. An attractive acquisition possibility is available, but no one in his organization is able to evaluate the technical and economic advantages of the new technology critically, nor to determine whether the new technology could be assimilated easily by present manufacturing facilities and personnel.

C. The director of engineering of one division of a hundred-million-dollar-plus international corporation is consulting with the corporate vice president of engineering about whether a new generation of industrial drives should be designed using high-power silicon controlled rectifiers (SCR's). High-power SCR's are known to be in the prototype stage of development by several leading manufacturers, but it is not known whether the technical problems involved in large-scale production will result in a price structure so high as to make the new devices non-competitive with ones using existing technology.

These three problems are typical of several R&D decisions being successfully handled by a growing new management technique—the *technical board.*

---

*Reprinted with permission from *Michigan Business Review*, XIII, No. 2 (March, 1971), 11-15.

During the past five years we, the authors, have established a dozen such boards, and have served actively on many of them. The impetus to form the technical boards grew out of our involvement in devising means by which universities could become more effective in helping industry assimilate new technical developments associated with large scale university research efforts.

The Objectives

The basic objective of the technical board is to assume responsibility for maintaining the technical health of the corporation. In this role, the technical board functions in a restricted scope much like a corporate board of directors, which assumes responsibility for all aspects of the corporate health. The technical board, however, does not have legal responsibility as does the corporate board. However, the chairman of the technical board generally does have corporate responsibility for all technical activites. The technical board attempts to insure that the proper technical resources, both human and material, are employed to meet the corporate objectives. It is therefore concerned that technical personnel have proper initial and continuing training and are equipped with adequate facilities.

The elimination of the occurrence of technical surprises to the corporation is an important subsidiary objective. This has two key aspects: (1) adequate surveillance of technical developments generally, and (2) the choice of the best technical alternative, given the objectives and resources available to the corporation.

In this role, the board functions as a technical resource itself. Should the board not feel adequately qualified technically on a specific technical issue, it would have the responsibility to seek additional expert counsel to resolve the issue.

The objectives and duties of the board are similar to those Quinn described earlier as "science advisory committees," a procedure for technological forecasting.[1] He reported the use of such committees as one organizational approach which companies were experimenting with about the time our first technical boards were established.

> Science advisory committees are usually made up of eminent university or government scientists from a wide range of disciplines. The scientists offer advice to either the top executive's office or the company's chief technical officer. The committees typically meet not more than semiannually and/or on special request. Their functions are to help evaluate proposed science programs in fields new to the company, to ensure that the R&D program stays current in the committee members' fields of expertise, to advise on the overall balance of the company's research program, and to serve as an objective sounding board for company scientists and executives on specific scientific questions. They thus provide assistance in evaluating the potential worth and relevance of specific scientific fields to the company's future.[2]

---

[1]James Brian Quinn, "Technological Forecasting," *Harvard Business Review*, March-April, 1967, p. 103.
[2]*Ibid.*

Our present concept of the technical board, however, has evolved toward a greater degree of involvement with more frequent meetings and a greater sense of responsibility on the part of board members than had the members of the science advisory committee described by Quinn. The mix of equal numbers on inside and outside members on technical boards, described below, reflects this tendency toward involvement.

Why the Need

The need for the technical board stems basically from the generally accelerated pace of technological advance, which has been an outgrowth of federally sponsored research programs during and following World War II. Although most U.S. firms have not been heavily involved in such research, none have escaped its direct impact. For example, machine tool firms long accustomed to a creeping pace of technological change, must almost over night assimilate effectively the technology of electronic computer control and new methods of measurement, such as laser metrology.

Although this is an extreme case, the same task of assimilating technical change exists in firms in all industries. And those in an industry with a modern technological base, such as electronics or scientific instruments, now face a plethora of technical alternatives. As another instance, the success of the small manufacturer of remote access computer terminals depends on the wisdom of the selection from many alternatives in solid-state logic, memory, and keyboard devices.

The basic need is felt not only by small and medium-sized firms (although the payoff from a technical board is perhaps greatest for these), but by large firms as well. No matter how large the firm, it cannot economically be on top of every technical development. The stakes in proper choice among available alternatives are so high that such firms, too, can profit from independent, objective appraisal of the alternatives.

The Composition, Organization, and Term of the Board

"Tailor made" is the appropriate label for every technical board organized to date. In one respect, however, they are similar. Each board includes about equal numbers of inside and outside members. To give continuity and effectiveness to the board, outside members are generally asked to serve at least a two- or three-year term, the same as inside members. The selection of outside members depends on the nature of current technical problems and the product directions in which the company is headed. Inside members generally include the vice president of research, and/or director(s) of engineering, and key scientific research personnel. The number of outside people required on a board depends on the breadth of technologies covered by the firm. To date, the number has ranged from a minimum of two outside men for a firm with sales of less than $5 million dollars to a maximum of eight representing several universities for a large multidivisional firm. This basic group then brings in other technical experts when needed on special issues. Experience with the boards has also led to the inclusion of one inside and one outside member who is not strictly a technical expert but is a professional in product planning or marketing. This is a result of the realization that proper long-range market guidance is a necessity for efficient and profitable employment of technical resources.[3]

The Line of Authority

The best source of outside personnel to serve on the boards usually has been a university where professors are actively engaged in frontier research or consulting. It is not that others in industry, or in private research laboratories are not technically qualified, but rather it is that they are more likely to be involved in applied research of a proprietary nature and might soon encounter conflicts of interest. This has been our experience to date. Such personnel are, however, most useful as adjunct expert counsel on isolated technical issues. To date, we have employed university faculty from The University of Michigan, Michigan State University, Ohio State University, Case Western Reserve, and Notre Dame University on technical boards in the Midwest.

In about half the cases (usually in small firms), a line executive officer at the vice-presidential level is a member and chairman of the board. In other instances the vice president for research is a member and chairman of the board. Every board also has a university member as co-chairman or coordinator to maintain liaison with the company, coordinate the efforts of university personnel, help plan the agenda, and arrange for special experts. The university coordinator has proven to be necessary to keep the board functioning smoothly.

The Mode of Operation

The pattern of operation has evolved as follows. The need to solve some immediate technical problem generally provides the impetus to form the board. The primary attention has then been directed toward the solution of the problem at hand.

With the successful resolution of the immediate problem, the second step is to begin a systematic review of existing products, facilities, and research projects. This review provides a means for inside and outside members to become better acquainted, and to identify broadly the technical areas which need to be examined more closely.

The third step is to establish the priority for each technical area to be examined. An inside board member is then generally assigned the task of preparing a briefing on the subject chosen for the next meeting of the board. After the board has received the briefing, it may resolve the issue then and there, or it may assign someone to obtain additional information. Often at this stage, an outside member will be assigned to assist the inside member in broadening the field of inquiry. This may involve consultation

---

[3]McGlauchlin emphasizes this point as one of his main conclusions from his technical planning work at Honeywell. See Lawrence D. McGlauchlin, "Long-Range Technical Planning," *Harvard Business Review*, July-August, 1968, p. 64.

240

with experts who have specialized in the subject. The procedure continues until the issue is resolved or at least the state of ignorance is thoroughly documented. At this point, the board may recommend initiation of a research program or, if this is too costly for the company, the board may recommend a passive monitoring of the research activities of other organizations.

The systematic review of all products and research projects may take three to six months in a small company, with meetings twice a month for the first three months and once a month thereafter. In a large company with meetings on the same schedule, the review may take a year or more, partly because new topics often arise before the initial review is completed and are handled concomitantly.

After all projects have been reviewed, the board generally meets once every two months. Half the agenda is devoted to a briefing on a new technical field of potential interest to the corporation by an outside expert not regularly on the board. Often, other members of the corporate management or research staff may be invited to such briefings. One of the duties of the outside board members is to alert the corporation to such new developments and to arrange for such briefings.

Special meetings of the technical board can be called whenever a key technical issue must be resolved quickly. The board also frequently assists in acquisition and merger analyses by evaluating the technical strength of potential corporate candidates. In these several ways the members of the board discharge their prime responsibility: the maintenance of the present and future technological health of the corporation.

The Cost

The total annual cost for the outside members of the board has generally been about equal to the cost of one of the corporation's top scientific or technical men. In a small company this may be about $15,000 to $20,000 per year, and in a very large company it may amount to about $30,000 to $40,000 per year. Outside members are paid on a consulting basis by the corporation either individually or through a contract between the corporation and the university. In the latter case, the contract covers the cost of continuing liaison. Large corporations have generally preferred this option. Small firms, however, usually prefer individual arrangements where one outside member is additionally employed to maintain the liaison and coordination. The economic benefit of the technique is simply this: for the price of one top researcher, the corporation obtains continuing assistance, as needed, from six to twelve top men on a consulting basis.

Problems Encountered

Despite the success of the technical board concept, there are problems in its administration. Three main difficulties have been encountered to date.

There has been some fear on the part of management that the outsiders may divulge the special technical knowledge that the firm has developed or has under development. Second, there have been the human problems of suspicion of outsiders and resistance to the acceptance of constructive criticism. Third, there has been some difficulty in maintaining the continuity of the board when the chief executive officer on the board has been promoted or leaves the company.

The first problem is fortunately minimized by using university technical personnel. Besides their respect for proprietary rights, they are generally interested in fundamental problems associated with basic research, and are thus unlikely to have a professional interest in specific applied research results or product developments.

The second problem is mitigated by using only first-class technical men as members of the board. Their technical competence commands the natural respect of industry engineers and scientists. On the other hand, many of the best technical personnel are not known for their personal diplomacy. Careful selection of the university personnel helps, but frequently a brilliant but not-too-tactful scientist needs to be brought in. In this case, the university liaison member must adequately prepare key industry personnel and assist with added diplomacy when needed.

The third problem, the maintenance of continuity with change in the corporate chairman of the technical board, has been faced in four instances to date. In one of the cases, the board was maintained intact by the successor. In a second instance the board was temporarily dissolved but later reinstated, and in the other two cases, the board has not been continued to date. This problem of continuity does not exist with the corporate general board of directors because that board, of course, remains when the chief executive officer retires or takes a position elsewhere. However, in the case of the technical board, the board is designed to meet the special technical needs of the corporation, which to a considerable extent are those viewed as such by the chief technical officer. Consequently a new officer may view the needs differently, and not being familiar with the operation of a technical board, may consider that it is unnecessary. As the technique becomes more widely understood, this problem of continuity should become less serious. The fact that two of the cases mentioned have already survived such transition suggests this will be the condition.

In addition to the direct benefits to the firms and the remuneration which outside board members receive, there are several other by-product benefits to both. The university professor becomes aware of the applied problems in his field and can bring the knowledge gained back to the classroom. Firms, in turn, have a better understanding of the university and especially how to better use this resource. For example, one large firm sent a team of its researchers to work in a specially equipped university holography laboratory to learn how the new technology might be applied to their problems, without having to make the expensive capital equipment outlay.

Conclusions

Results with technical boards that have been formed and operated within the past five years indicate a solid pattern of success. The greatest success has resulted in small firms whose management has energetically

242

implemented the recommendations of the technical board. Success of the technical boards has also been enhanced by improvement in long-range product planning procedures, which were also implemented on the recommendation of the technical board as a means to improve performance of the technical R&D function.